# A SINKING NATION

## UNRAVELING THE COMPLEXITIES OF THE
## OF THE
## U.S. DEBT AND DEFICIT

*A Sinking Nation*

Published by Dei Saphan LLC
3425 Cliff Shadows Parkway, Suite 110A
Las Vegas, NV 89129

Cover Design and Illustrations by Tim O'Brien

ISBN: 978-0-69276-477-0

*Dedicated to Michelle, Grier, Reagan and Suzie*

*The Leading Ladies of my life*

# TABLE OF CONTENTS

# ACKNOWLEDGEMENTS

Numerous people have contributed in some manner to the completion of this project. I'm grateful for all of you, but there are a few individuals I want to specifically commend.

Words can't express my appreciation for my loving wife, Michelle. I could not have chosen a better spouse and partner for life. She has supported and believed in me, even when I didn't believe in myself.

My mother, Suzie, was my lifelong cheerleader. Sadly, she closed the final chapter of her life shortly before the book was published. She would have been proud, irrespective of how many people read my work.

*A Sinking Nation* would not be nearly as good without the diligence and help of my wonderful editor, Lori Handelman, and illustrator, Tim O'Brien. Lori's differing opinions and perspective have made me and this book better. The illustrations Tim developed are more effective than a thousand words in depicting the magnitude of the issues addressed.

Trey Pecor is a wonderful friend, and the inspiration for this project came from a casual meeting with him a few years ago. I'm grateful for Adam Alpert, who provided honest feedback on the manuscript and offered an endorsement for others to read it, too.

There are many friends who have supported me through this process, but I need to give special thanks to Paul Goulet, Jon Ponder, Randy Tatano and Phil Zaldatte for their additional efforts getting this book to print.

# FOREWORD

The deficit and mounting Federal debt have been talking points in politics for many years. The public's vague notion that the present level of borrowing is bad and probably unsustainable has been recognized by many savvy candidates as a hot button issue to be exploited on the campaign trail for decades. But once the campaign is over and the candidate elected, a curious thing happens: spending increases and the debt grows.

In *A Sinking Nation*, Marshall addresses both the root causes and history of the debt crisis in the United States. Much of his focus is on demystifying the special language politicians use to obfuscate the budgeting process—especially the way congressionally mandated scoring rules like baseline budgeting often label true budget increases as budget decreases for public consumption. Marshall also clearly explains the many convoluted methodologies employed to finance debt, and how some partitioned trust fund surpluses, like the Social Security Trust Fund, may not be as safe as publically advertised.

This book is quite sobering. Although not offering specific remedies, Marshall makes a compelling argument that a confluence of factors including rising interest rates, an aging population, and unfettered spending could lead to a catastrophe like what happened in Greece, and in the not-too-future.

*A Sinking Nation* will be the go-to book for experts and layman seeking commonsense explanations of the United States' deficit and debt. It is written in an engaging style, demonstrating Marshall's mastery of the subject and ability to communicate a complex topic in a lucid way. A great read!

Adam Alpert
Vice-President and Director of BioTek Instruments, Inc.

# INTRODUCTION

⌁⌁⌁

A Sunken Ship

On April 10, 1912, the mooring lines were dropped from the Southampton, England pier and the propellers churned the harbor waters as the ship slowly got under way. An air of excitement permeated the dock and the vessel. Passengers and crew knew they were making history by being on the maiden voyage of a new luxury liner, the *RMS Titanic*.

The *Titanic* made two ports of call before striking out for New York: Cherbourg, France and Queenstown, Ireland. When the *Titanic* steamed out of Cork Harbor on April 11, the 2,208 people aboard had no idea the fateful events they would experience 84 hours later.

For three days, the ship sailed across the North Atlantic without incident and was set to sail into New York Harbor on schedule. Everything changed at 11:40pm on April 14 when the *Titanic* struck an iceberg. The initial damage assessment was underestimated; however, it didn't take long for everyone on board to realize the supposedly unsinkable ship was sinking fast, and doom was imminent. In fewer than three hours, the mighty *Titanic* plunged to the ocean floor 12,000 feet below the surface, taking the lives of 1,503 people in the process. Sadly, more than twice as many people perished as survived.

1

Survivors described the chaos on board after the ship struck the iceberg. Passengers and crew went from planning their arrival a few hours hence, to fighting for their lives.

Much time can be spent contemplating what might have happened if different actions had been taken. It's fruitless to speculate about potential outcomes, but there were a number of decisions which accelerated the ship's sinking and increased the loss of life.

- 1,178 lifeboat seats were on board for 2,208 people (only 962 were required by law).

- After spotting the iceberg, the officer of the watch reversed the engines, thus slowing her motion. Since ships turn more quickly at faster speeds, it's possible the ship could have avoided the iceberg completely without this maneuver.

- The ship was cruising at 22.5 knots. Its top speed was 23.0 knots.

- The *Titanic* received and ignored six ice warnings throughout the day on April 14.

- The watertight compartments had openings at the top, allowing water to flood into other areas of the ship.[1]

Some conclusions can be drawn from these few facts. Most notably, the pervasive attitude of the *Titanic*'s crew was hubris. The mere idea of an unsinkable ship affected the crew's decision to ignore the multiple ice warnings and continue cruising at top speed. It also affected the company's decision to limit the number of lifeboat seats, even though the ship had 216 more seats than required by law. It was common belief at the time that lifeboats were only needed to shuttle people from one ship to another, not to keep every person onboard afloat simultaneously. However, as the ship sank in the middle of the night, nearly half of the people didn't have a seat in a lifeboat and were forced into the icy waters of the North Atlantic.

Decisions were made which affected the outcome long before the ship ever touched water. As an example, the design flaw of the watertight compartments may not have prevented the *Titanic* from sinking, but it likely hastened the ship's demise. In the end, the fate of more than 2,200 people was determined by a few people (e.g., the captain, the officer of the watch, the wireless operator, and the design engineers).

A Sinking Nation

There are dramatic differences between the *Titanic* and the fiscal affairs of the United States government, but parallels can be drawn.

America is a great nation, and it has occupied a unique place in the world over the past century. Since the end of the Second World War, the United States has been an unrivaled superpower in the world. Undoubtedly there are other great nations, but what other nation has experienced the same consistent global political influence, economic strength, and military power over the past 60 years?

It has not always been smooth sailing, and our nation and economy have weathered many storms. Somehow we managed to make it through the oil embargo and stagflation years of the 1970s; the savings and loan crisis of the late 1980s; the bursting of the tech bubble in the late 1990s; the terrorist attacks of September 11, 2001; and the Great Recession of 2008 and 2009 involving the collapse of the U.S. real estate market.

Our ability to survive is a testament to the resiliency of our country and economy, but it can lead to a sense of complacency and arrogance—probably a lot like the attitudes of people aboard the *Titanic* as she set sail for America. There are some obvious indicators of danger lurking on the horizon for our nation. If we ignore the signals, as the *Titanic* crew disregarded the ice warnings, we too could find ourselves in the midst of an unexpected tragedy . . . largely of our own making.

The sinking of the *Titanic* was a tragic accident, and one can only speculate whether it was avoidable. Even though the iceberg could be considered an act of nature, icebergs are not uncommon in the North Atlantic during April, and in fact the crew was made aware of their presence. Engineering flaws and operational decisions certainly contributed to the ship's demise.

A similar assessment could be made if the U.S. meets a future financial calamity. Like an iceberg looming in the dark waters, political or economic events in other parts of the world may trigger a financial collapse, but it won't be the sole cause of our downfall. The chronic overspending and debt accumulated over the past 60 years will have severely weakened our ability to cope with such an event. We can blame politicians, but we the people must bear some responsibility since we enabled them through our votes.

Political Power

In that respect, millions of Americans are like the *Titanic* passengers who entrusted their future to a few decision makers, most whom they didn't even know. The U.S. is a democratic republic. Except for referendums and constitutional measures, voters elect representatives to make laws and decisions. You may not have voted for the decision makers, but a majority of voters did. Whether you agree with them or not, they are making decisions that affect your daily life.

Although politics has always been somewhat unsavory, it seems to be continually more repulsive. There may be many contributing factors, but many can be summarized as (1) the desire to gain and retain power, and (2) the privileges of power.

Campaigns are supposed to provide a presentation of ideas for voters to decide who they want to lead, and the policies they want to pursue. Campaign mudslinging has always existed, but the process seems to have gotten more vitriolic and divisive, as candidates seem less focused on the exchange of ideas and more on personal attacks. This was on clear display during the 2012 Presidential election. For example, Democratic Senate Majority Leader, Senator Harry Reid (arguably the most powerful Senator in the U.S. at the time), stood on the floor of the Senate and accused former Republican Governor Mitt Romney of not paying taxes for the previous ten years. His claim was later proven false. When asked about it after the election, Senator Reid's response was, "Romney didn't win did he."[2]

I think Americans expect and are willing to accept a certain level of political posturing and spin, but the process has devolved into an environment where political ends justify the means. Unfortunately, such antics erode confidence in our leaders, leaving it difficult to trust the people we elect. Senator Reid and the Democrats are not alone in their tactics to gain and retain power, but this is an example of the rhetoric and tactics employed in modern campaigns.

I witnessed a simple example of the privileges of power a couple years ago when I was on the same international flight as Republican Senator John McCain. Senator McCain and his aide were segregated from the rest of the passengers waiting to board, and no one else was allowed to board until they were situated in their first class seats. Upon arrival in the U.S., two U.S. Border and Customs officers met them at the gate and personally escorted them through the terminal, bypassing the immigration checkpoint. Certainly, Senator McCain had better things to do with his time than stand in line waiting to clear immigration, but the same can be said of many frequent business travelers who have spent hours languishing in lines waiting to clear immigration or security checkpoints. This may seem like a trivial matter, but it's an example of how our elected officials create special benefits and exceptions to laws for themselves.

Within the halls of Congress, seniority and longevity equate to power, and the more power you have, the more benefits you can bestow upon your constituents and yourself. Many of the sitting senators and representatives have served in Congress for decades.

They have become career politicians. As in all professions, there are benefits to wisdom and experience; however, there are also drawbacks to serving in Washington for so long and being isolated from the routines of average citizens. As my anecdote about Senator McCain suggests, it's difficult for leaders to understand the frustrations of airport security when they are able to bypass it. As for Senator Reid's behavior, it's indicative of what people will do to hold the levers of power, including passing laws (e.g., gerrymandering) to prevent an opponent from unseating you.

In sum, the system has created a political aristocracy. It's an environment where our leaders often speak about doing what's best for their constituents, but they often act in a manner that serves their own political and financial interests. The result is an increasing distrust of our elected officials and their motives. This phenomenon may be applicable to many different aspects of governing, but the coming chapters will reveal how our leaders are often less than honest or forthcoming when discussing the fiscal affairs of our nation. You will also discover how they are using the funds in the U.S. Treasury to gain and retain power.

## Exploiting Complexity

Without being overly cynical, I believe our political leaders have exploited the complexity of the government and the budgetary process for their personal political advantage. By keeping voters in the dark through obscure language and political spin, they have used the U.S. Treasury for their pet projects, pork barrel spending, and tax breaks to bolster their chances for re-election, thereby further increasing their political power and influence.

Politicians aren't sinister, they're just politicians. They have mastered the art of parsing words and telling voters what they want to hear. There is a lot of talk about holding our elected officials accountable, but it's hard to hold anyone accountable without good information. Don't expect accurate information to come from politicians, especially if it portrays them in a negative light.

Except for a few details involving certain classified matters, government finances are a matter of public record. However, open access doesn't equate to widespread or easy dissemination. The information is there, but you have to dig for it. Since the issues can be complex and abstract, it's difficult to condense them into 15-second sound bites and brief news segments.

Sadly, most fiscal conversations are dominated by partisans with a political agenda. As a result, the information is presented in a manner to lead you towards a specific conclusion. Like any other person, I have opinions and biases, but I have made my best attempt to present the information on the debt and deficit in an apolitical manner.

Toward this objective, you will not find specific solutions to the challenges we face. This is intentional. Once possible solutions are offered, the discussion seems to quickly evolve into ideological and political debates. My personal ideas and opinions are not the focus of this book. My goal instead is to provide you with information to help develop your own ideas, rather than pontificating and defending mine.

## Keep It Simple

With a $3.5 trillion budget, scores of departments and agencies, and millions of employees, the U.S. government is one of the largest enterprises on earth. Given the immense size, no single person is knowledgeable about every aspect of the budget—not even those employed full-time to manage it. Fortunately, you don't need to comprehend every detail of the budget to understand and discuss budgetary issues. By applying common sense and basic financial principles to some key financial metrics, you can have a rudimentary understanding of the fiscal policies and situation of the U.S. government.

Although the numbers are exponential compared to your personal finances, managing the government's money is not very different than managing your own. However, some really smart people and so-called experts can recite a host of reasons why simple financial principles don't apply to federal spending. While there are differences and exceptional circumstances, the basic principles still apply over the long term. For instance, a simple concept parents teach their children is not to spend more than you make. The loss of your job or an unexpected emergency might cause you to spend more than you make in a given year, but you know you can't sustain that approach forever. If perpetual overspending is bad for you, how is it good for the federal government?

The following chapters will unravel some of these complexities and present information in a manner that is comprehensible for the average citizen. In addition to a number of charts, graphs and illustrations, you will read a lot of analogies. Even though the comparisons won't be exact, I believe they will bring clarity to a number of topics which might otherwise seem obtuse.

## Qualifications

Honestly, one of the biggest hurdles I encountered in writing this book was evaluating whether I am qualified to write on this topic. I'll briefly state my case.

I have been a practicing Certified Public Accountant (CPA) for more than 25 years, specializing in tax planning and compliance for entrepreneurs and high net worth families. There are thousands of pages of IRS laws and regulations on these topics, plus volumes of court cases and rulings. Tax law is complex, and at times extremely confusing. For years I have explained complex tax rules in a manner that is understandable for clients who need to make financial decisions. In this book I rely on a similar approach to explaining the debt, deficit and other fiscal policy topics.

Charts, graphs and other visual illustrations are very helpful in communicating complex topics or structures, even for people who are very good with numbers. Analogies, even if imperfect, are useful in placing a principle within a familiar context so you can apply the principle to other situations. Therefore, you will find extensive use of charts, graphs, illustrations and analogies throughout the rest of this book. Although it may be challenging to understand some of the topics, it's possible if we stick to basic financial principles and common sense.

## A Simple Approach

This book is not written for academics, policy wonks or Washington insiders. It's written for the average American citizen desiring a simple explanation of the financial status of our nation. Some so-called experts may act as if these issues are beyond the grasp of the average citizen, but they are wrong. Since the Constitution and Bill of Rights were primarily written as restrictions on government power, I don't believe the Founding Fathers ever intended for the government to be too complex for the average citizen to understand. Consequently, I think every citizen has the right and responsibility to understand the fiscal policies and financial status of our government, and I believe *A Sinking Nation* will increase your awareness and understanding.

For some readers, this book will seem like an overly simplistic explanation of the issues we face. Discussing topics in simple terms doesn't negate their complexity or the challenge of finding workable solutions, but in my experience, simplifying that which is complex makes a solution more attainable. If we always think about the complexity of the problems, the solutions will forever seem evasive. Let's be honest. If it were easy to fix our financial situation, it would have already been done. At the same time, even though it may be difficult, we can make changes to fix our problems and secure the financial future of our nation.

Join the Conversation

The financial matters of the federal government are beyond a single person's ability to comprehend. Similarly, the solutions to our problems are bigger than any one person's ability to resolve, even the President. It's going to take cooperation among a disparate group of people.

Because we live under a representative form of government, you may never have the opportunity to vote on a particular measure addressing the budget or the deficit, but you can still be involved. You don't need a huge platform to make a difference. Increasing your knowledge, sharing with others, and voting to support candidates who are serious about addressing our fiscal situation is an excellent start.

Hopefully, this book will help inform and inspire you to join the conversation. If you take the time and make it a priority for our nation to address our long-term fiscal problems, we can only have faith others will too.

Ready to join the conversation? Let's start by exploring some of the jargon and terminology used in discussing the debt and deficit.

# CHAPTER 1
# LEARN THE LINGO

In your quest to better understand and discuss topics related to the debt and deficit, you need to learn the lingo. Even if you have a good grasp of the terminology, a quick refresher might be in order.

Politicians, political operatives, and pundits may not lie or intentionally deceive people, but they are good at "spinning." Spinning is the ability to present something in a certain way for the reader or listener to draw an intended conclusion. The spin masters extract certain facts or details which support their position, and ignore facts and circumstances contradictory to their position. Consequently, understanding the terminology will help you understand a person's position or proposal.

**Debt** – This is the total amount of money borrowed by the U.S. government from individuals, corporations, foreign governments, the U.S. Federal Reserve System, and other agencies of the federal government (e.g., the Social Security Trust Fund). As of December 31, 2015, the U.S. debt was approximately $18.9 trillion, which is more than $56,000 for every person in the United States. Check www.usdebtclock.org for an updated tally.

**Deficit** – The amount the U.S. government spends in excess of the revenues it collects. For fiscal year 2015, the deficit was approximately $438 billion, and the 2016deficit is projected to be $616 billion. The largest annual deficit was recorded in fiscal 2009: a whopping $1.4 trillion.

**Fiscal Year** – The U.S. government accounts for its income and expenses using a fiscal year of October 1 through September 30. The budget year references the end of the fiscal period for which it relates; for example, the 2015 Budget covers the period of October 1, 2014 through September 30, 2015.

**Budget** –The budget is an agreement by the House and Senate establishing overall revenue and spending parameters for the fiscal year. The budget is effectively a blueprint that guides congressional committees as to how much revenue must be raised and the amount of money which can be spent by each department and agency.

**Appropriations** – Article 1, Section 9, Clause 7 of the U.S. Constitution states, "No Money shall be drawn from the Treasury, but in Consequence of Appropriations made by Law..." Congress must pass and the President must sign legislation authorizing the expenditure of federal monies. Under the current legislative process, there are twelve different appropriation bills which cover all federal spending, except for special or emergency appropriations. The twelve appropriation bills constitute the spending portion of the budget and fund the various departments and operations of the government (e.g., Agriculture, Defense, Homeland Security, and Transportation). Revenues are generated from taxes and other fees collected by the federal government and passed in separate legislation from the annual appropriation bills. For political purposes, Congress often combines several (or all) of the spending bills into an omnibus spending bill. This is a political maneuver to force members of both parties to vote for things they don't like in order to get the things they support.

**Continuing Resolution** – When Congress is unable to pass the necessary budget and appropriation bills, they will often pass a continuing resolution to keep the government functioning. The continuing resolution is a temporary measure intended to maintain government operations until Congress and the President enact the necessary appropriations legislation.

**Debt Ceiling or Debt Limit** – Article 1, Section 8 of the U.S. Constitution states that Congress shall have the power "To borrow Money on the credit of the United States." Prior to 1917, Congress voted and approved each issuance of debt by the U.S. Treasury. During World War I, Congress passed the Second Liberty Bond Act, which authorized the U.S. Treasury to issue debt obligations up to a stated aggregate amount. This aggregate borrowing limit has been dubbed the "debt ceiling." With the passage of the Bipartisan Budget Act of 2015 in November 2015, the current debt ceiling was suspended until March 16, 2017.[3] Once the debt ceiling has been reached, the Treasury is precluded from borrowing additional money from investors or other governmental agencies.

**Mandatory (Entitlement) Spending** – Mandatory spending is still governed by federal law, but it does not require the passage of an annual appropriations bill. Social Security, Medicare and Medicaid constitute virtually all mandatory spending by the U.S. government. The level of spending is dictated by the most recent law determining eligibility. Persons who meet the requirements are entitled to the benefits provided, resulting in the moniker of "entitlement programs."

**Discretionary Spending** – All expenditures by the U.S. government are dictated by federal law. Discretionary spending is classified as all spending other than mandatory spending and interest on the outstanding debt. It is covered by the various annual appropriations bills passed by Congress. The general parameters of federal spending are determined by the House and Senate Appropriations Committees. Discretionary spending requires an annual vote by Congress.

**CBO (Congressional Budget Office)** – The CBO was created in 1974[4] and is intended to be a nonpartisan agency of the legislative branch. Its primary purpose is assisting Congress with fiscal and budgetary matters. The three primary functions of the CBO are providing budgetary projections for Congress to pass the required budgetary and appropriations legislation, re-estimating the President's budget, and estimating the revenues and expenditures of every piece of legislation passed by a House or Senate committee.

**OMB (Office of Management and Budget)** – The OMB is a cabinet-level office of the Executive Branch. Its primary purpose is to prepare the President's budget and supervise its administration within the various executive agencies. In formulating the budget, the OMB evaluates the effectiveness of agency programs and policies and sets funding priorities based upon the President's policy goals and objectives. Like most agencies of the Executive Branch, there is a mixture of political appointees and career staff, with the senior leaders being political appointees.

**Baseline Budgeting** – Baseline budgeting is a budgetary methodology used by the U.S. government to project future spending. Current spending provides a baseline for estimating future expenditures. The methodology assumes the current fiscal policies and spending will continue for the next ten years, with guaranteed increases for inflation and population growth. The current baseline increases for mandatory expenditures are estimated at 5.63%.[5] Thus, if the U.S. government spends $1 million dollars on a particular program, it's automatically assumed to spend 5.63% more for each of the next ten years. Under these assumptions, spending will repeatedly increase from $1,000,000 to $1,729,310 over the decade. Spending more than the baseline is classified as a spending increase, and spending less qualifies as a spending cut.

**Scoring** – The CBO acts as the official scorekeeper of Congressional spending, and it reports whether legislation meets the revenue and expenditure guidelines established by Congress. The process of estimating the net revenue or cost of legislation is referred to as scoring. In an era of trillion dollar deficits and debt, the CBO scoring process has become increasingly important. In light of a Congressional goal for legislation to be deficit neutral, the CBO score of proposed legislation is often a factor in determining whether a particular bill can garner sufficient votes to pass the House and Senate.

**Budget Period** – This is not a specific term you will hear discussed, but it's one of the most important aspects of the discussion regarding the budget, taxes and spending. The U.S. government has a 12-month annual budget. The CBO scores revenue and expenditures on a ten-year horizon. Politicians frequently use these budget periods interchangeably to create a favorable perception of their positions and policies. For example, an official may state that he or she helped cut the deficit by $1 trillion. Since total current federal spending is approximately $3.5 trillion annually, there is no way spending was reduced by nearly one-third, so in this case the person is talking about spending reductions over the next ten years. Furthermore, depending upon how the legislation is written, the spending cuts could be back-loaded (i.e., the cuts happen in years 8-10). Thus, the person has created an impression that spending reductions are taking place when in fact, nothing has changed. In an extreme scenario, spending may increase in the short-term, with larger reductions planned for the future. By the time the scheduled changes are implemented, new legislation could be enacted to prevent the cuts from occurring, but initial legislation will still be scored as a spending cut by the CBO. It's unlikely a politician will specifically state the budget period to which they are referring, so you must differentiate the annual budget period from the CBO ten-year budget projection to comprehend what is actually being proposed or discussed.

**Bond Rating** – A bond credit rating is assigned to a particular debt instrument, which indicates the financial strength of the issuer and the likelihood the investor will receive the scheduled payments of interest and principal. Credit ratings are assigned by independent ratings agencies, such as Fitch Ratings, Moody's, and Standard & Poor's. Bond ratings are designated by a letter or combination of letter and numbers, indicating the investment quality of the bond. The credit rating has no direct connection to the interest rate or payment terms of the bond, but the bond rating will often impact a bond's trading price on the public market.

**Treasury Department** – The U.S. Treasury Department is a cabinet-level agency under the direction of the Secretary of the Treasury. Like the OMB, Treasury employs a mixture of political appointees and career civil employees, with political appointees occupying the senior leadership roles. The Treasury has a variety of responsibilities including: collecting taxes (the Internal Revenue Service is part of the Treasury Department); paying the bills of the federal government; managing currency and coins; issuing U.S. government debt securities and servicing the public debt; supervising certain banks and financial institutions; and advising the President on economic, monetary, tax and trade policies.

## Listen Carefully

Understanding terminology is important to com-prehending conversations in any profession, activity or arena of life. Learning the lingo of federal finances will help as you read this book, but more importantly, it will help you discern what politicians are really saying when they speak about the budget, debt, and deficit.

Once you understand the terminology, you will discover that politicians often use terms interchangeably to create certain impressions. For example, the words debt and deficit are frequently used synonymously. A political speech may make several references to reducing the debt and cutting the deficit. Speakers may reference reducing the debt, which gives the impression they are going to reduce the $18 trillion national debt. In reality, they are talking about reducing the annual deficit, which only slows the rate we're adding to the national debt. In our current situation, the government could cut the annual deficit in half and still add more than $300 billion to the national debt each year. It may be a step in the right direction, but the total debt still increased by $300 billion.

With a better understanding of the terminology and the clear distinction between the debt and the deficit, it's time to tackle specific issues. The debt is really an accumulation of spending deficits, so unraveling the deficit seems like a prerequisite to the discussion of the debt.

# CHAPTER 2
# THE DEFICIT

## Overview

A deficit occurs when there is a lack or shortage of something. A government budget deficit occurs when expenditures exceed revenues for a specific project or period of time. Congress passes an annual budget and corresponding legislation approving certain expenditures, and the various departments and agencies collect the appropriate taxes, fees, levies and income. A surplus is realized if the revenues exceed expenditures, and a deficit occurs when expenditures are greater than the income collected.

The size of the deficit has varied greatly. The smallest deficit was $1.2 billion in fiscal 1938, and the largest was recognized in fiscal 2009, more than $1.4 trillion. There are a great number of reasons for the budget deficits incurred, such as the Great Depression, economic recessions, and wars. There are also plenty of people responsible for continuous government overspending. Irrespective of the rationale or responsibility, the U.S. government clearly has a spending problem. The numbers speak for themselves. Excluding Social Security and other trust funds, the U.S. government has recognized a budget surplus seven times in the past 80 years. It has happened only once since 1960, in 2000. (See Table 1)

**U.S. Goverment Deficit**
**(millions of dollars)**

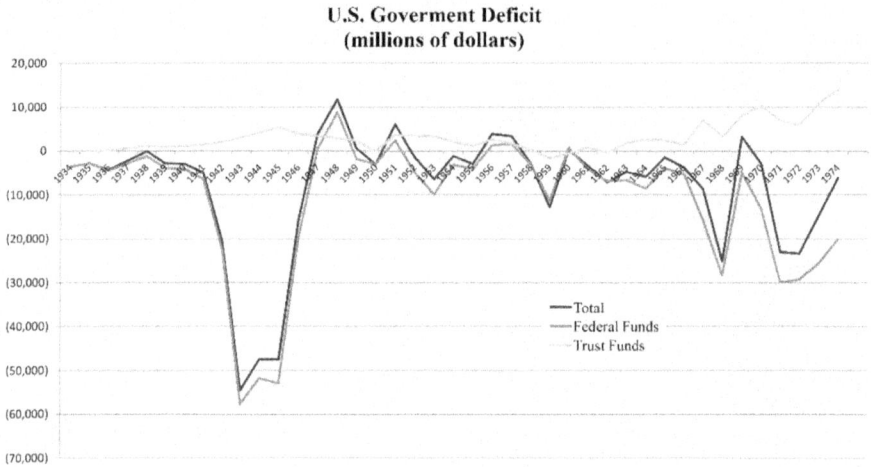

**U.S. Goverment Deficit**
**(millions of dollars)**

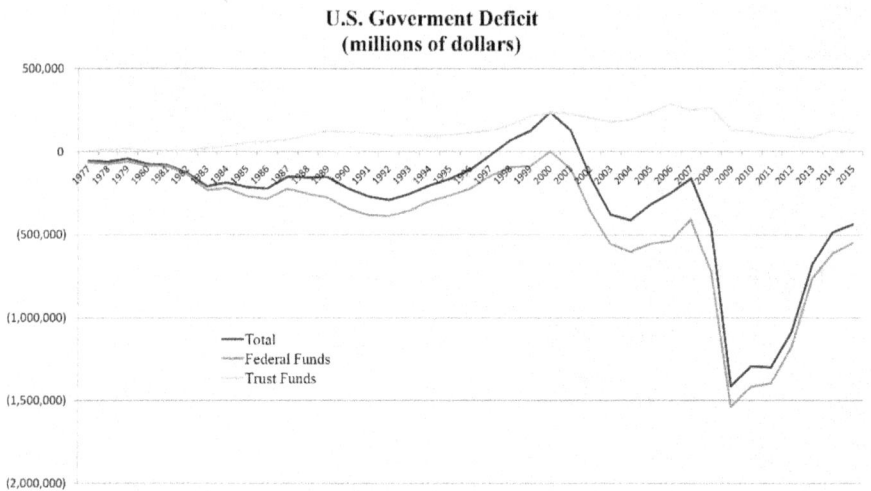

Source: http://www.whitehouse.gov/omb/budget/Historicals/

Overspending is undoubtedly a chronic problem in Washington rather than an isolated event.

Politicians always blame other people and political parties as being responsible for deficit spending, but nearly eight decades of overspending is not the fault of any particular person or party. In reality, there is plenty of blame and responsibility to share for our current fiscal situation. As depicted in the following illustration, it doesn't really matter which party controls Congress or the presidency; the federal government spends more than it receives.

**Deficit and the Balance of Power**

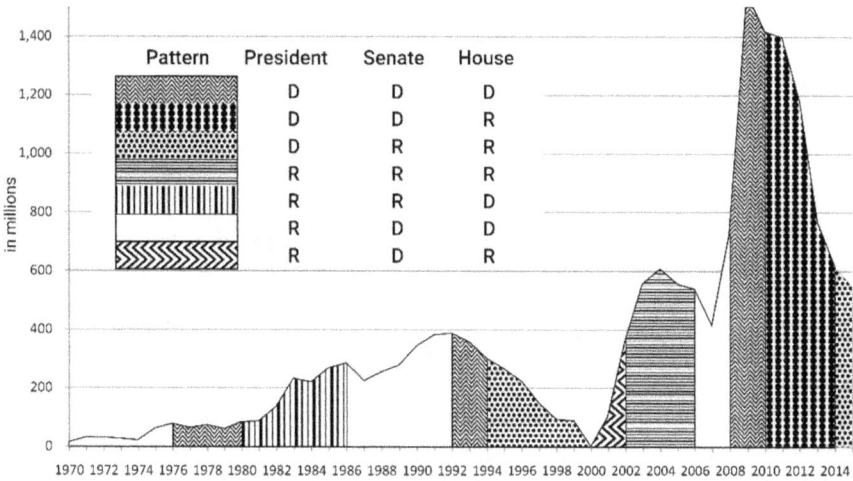

| Pattern | President | Senate | House |
|---|---|---|---|
| | D | D | D |
| | D | D | R |
| | D | R | R |
| | R | R | R |
| | R | R | D |
| | R | D | D |
| | R | D | R |

## The Budget Process

The annual U.S. budget is created through legislative process, which begins with the President delivering his budget request to Congress. His budget is developed by the OMB. According to the Budget and Accounting Act of 1921, the President delivers his proposed budget to the Congress between the last Monday in January and the first Monday in February.

Once received by Congress, the President's budget is scored by the CBO. The House and Senate also pass a concurrent budget resolution, which is essentially their response to the President's budget. As a congressional resolution, it doesn't have the force of law nor does it require the President's consent or signature. The budget resolution provides the parameters for all the other revenue and spending legislation considered by Congress. The budget resolution covers five years: the upcoming fiscal year, plus four subsequent years.

Under current congressional rules, twelve separate appropriations bills are passed:

1. Agriculture, Rural Development, Food and Drug Administration, and related agencies
2. Commerce, Justice, Science, and related agencies
3. Defense
4. Energy and Water Development, and related agencies
5. Financial Services and General Government
6. Homeland Security
7. Interior, Environment, and related agencies
8. Labor, Health and Human Services, Education, and related agencies
9. Legislative Branch
10. Military Construction, Veterans Affairs, and related agencies
11. State, Foreign Operations, and related programs
12. Transportation, Housing and Urban Development, and related agencies

In recent years, Congress has rarely passed all twelve bills. For political purposes, multiple bills (or all of them) have been combined into an omnibus spending bill.

Appropriations bills deal with spending. When Congress passes budget legislation, it effectively only controls the spending part of the equation. While the OMB and CBO provide estimates, the amount of revenues collected by the U.S. government is not exactly known. Although income tax rates and rules are controlled by Congress, the amount of tax revenue collected is determined by the amount of money individuals and corporations make during the year. The federal gas tax rate is fixed, but the gas tax revenue received by the Department of Transportation is determined by the amount of gas purchased. As a result, the revenue collected by the federal government is largely dependent upon the economic activity of the nation.

This differs from a municipal school budget, which collects a fixed amount of taxes by making an assessment against a predetermined list of property values. Since the municipality can more accurately determine the revenues collected, it's easier to determine whether the budget will be balanced. The only real uncertainty for revenues arises from delinquent or uncollectible taxes.

Since Congress essentially votes on the spending portion of the budget and not the revenue side, deficits can occur if actual revenues are less than projected. The uncertainty of revenues can contribute to the budget deficit for a particular period of time, but it doesn't account for eight decades of overspending. For most of the past 80 years, the deficit was intentional, not a surprise. There may not have been consensus on the magnitude or propriety of the deficit, but Congress and the President expected and agreed to deficit spending.

Revenue

Taxes are the federal government's primary source of income. Individual income, corporate income, Social Security, and Medicare comprise the majority of tax revenues. Table 2 shows the sources of revenue from 1940 to the present.

The U.S. Treasury collected $3.250 trillion in fiscal 2015. Income taxes provided 58% of the money collected, and Social Security and Medicare taxes comprised 33%.

**Fiscal 2015 Receipts by Source**

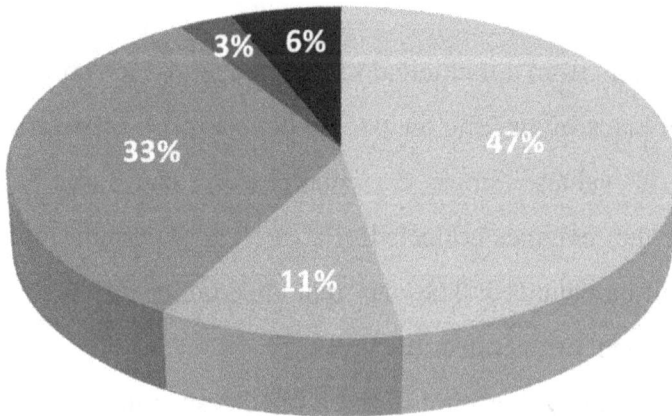

- Individual Income Taxes
- Corporate Income Taxes
- Social Insurance and Retirement Receipts
- Excise Taxes
- Other

Source: http://www.whitehouse.gov/omb/budget/Historicals/

Excise taxes are assessed for the purchase of a product, such as alcohol, tobacco and gasoline. Other receipts include estate and gift taxes, customs duties and fees for importing goods, and transfers from the Federal Reserve Bank. It also includes all other money received by the government: a few examples include royalties from oil and mineral rights, sale of federal land and buildings, and fines levied by various agencies (e.g., the Environmental Protection Agency and the Securities & Exchange Commission).

Table 2 also shows the allocable percentage of total revenue by source. The reliance upon individual income taxes and Social Security and Medicare taxes has increased over time. These two sources provided 41% of all federal revenues in 1940, and now provide more than 80%. Federal excise taxes have dropped from funding 30% of the government in 1940, to funding only 3%.

## Spending

Federal spending is classified into two broad categories: mandatory and discretionary. Other than interest on the national debt, no federal spending is really mandatory. However, Congress classifies mandatory spending as that which has been approved by some prior legislation. Although mandated by prior law, Congress could pass a new law revoking or revising the prior appropriation, but it rarely happens. Social Security, Medicare, and Medicaid account for the vast majority of mandatory spending, since the obligation for these payments was created by previous legislation.

As the term implies, discretionary spending is determined at the discretion of Congress with the consent of the President. The defense department receives approximately half of all discretionary spending. Since defending the country is one of the principal duties of the federal government, Congress is not likely to dramatically reduce defense spending in the near term. Therefore, a large portion of defense spending is effectively mandatory, even though it's classified as discretionary. The balance of discretionary spending operates the various government agencies, programs, and grants (e.g., agricultural subsidies, education, foreign aid, disaster relief and transportation).

The CBO and OMB track and report federal spending in multiple categories. The following classification is frequently used to categorize the nature of outlays by the U.S. government.

| Discretionary | Mandatory | Interest |
|---|---|---|
| Defense | Social Security | |
| Non-Defense | Medicare & Medicaid | |
| | Other Mandatory | |

## Fiscal 2015 Government Spending

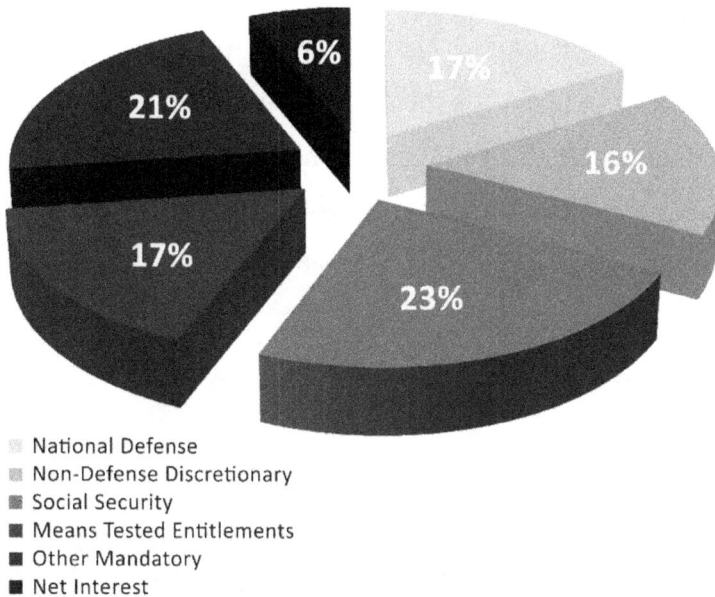

- National Defense
- Non-Defense Discretionary
- Social Security
- Means Tested Entitlements
- Other Mandatory
- Net Interest

Source: http://www.whitehouse.gov/omb/budget/Historicals/

There are pros and cons to mandatory spending. The primary benefit is derived by the recipients of the government payments. Mandatory spending assures people that the payments they were promised won't change every year based upon the political winds of Washington. The downside is that mandatory spending allows politicians to avoid casting politically unpopular votes by classifying something as mandatory. Rather than having to approve the current levels of spending each year, mandatory spending occurs automatically. Although Congress can modify mandatory expenditures by passing new legislation, they frequently act like it's beyond their control. As a result, the designated spending moves ahead unaltered.

It's not practical or wise to continually revise prior spending appropriations and promises, but there are times when it is prudent to revise previously approved appropriations which no longer may be necessary or affordable. It's the same thing you do with your personal finances. You don't change your cell phone or cable plan every month, but periodically you review your contracts and make changes. If finances are tight, you'll likely make changes to cut your bill, even if you've grown accustomed to certain features or made prior commitments to your family members. If you can do this, why shouldn't the U.S. government?

## Assets and Expenses

Under general principles of accounting, a distinction is made between annual operating expenses and the purchase of fixed assets which have a useful life over many years. For the U.S. government, no such distinction exists. Any money spent is treated as an annual expense, even the purchase of multi-billion dollar assets.

For example, a new F-35 fighter jet has an estimated cost in excess of $100 million dollars and may fly for decades.[6] For federal accounting budgetary purposes, the purchase of an F-35 is treated exactly the same as the cost of fuel for Air Force One, as a current expense.

Although this lack of capitalization can distort the long-term benefits of federal spending, it probably doesn't significantly alter the overall financial picture of the government. Even if the Air Force bought and paid for 200 new F-35 jets in one year, the cost is $20 billion. Not a small number, but it's only 0.6% of the $3.5 trillion the government spends in one year.

This failure to capitalize the purchase of long-term assets can distort the magnitude of the annual budget deficit, but it's only a timing issue. Over time, the majority of purchased assets will lose value, which is a true economic loss to the federal government. Recording all asset purchases as a current expense may distort the results for a particular year, but any distortion is eliminated after more than eight decades of continual deficit spending.

It may be a good accounting and theoretical argument to capitalize asset purchases instead of expensing them, but the recurring annual deficits are not the result of poor accounting policies and procedures.

## Entitlements and Mandatory Spending

Entitlement spending is often used synonymously with mandatory spending. Although there is some overlap, entitlements are different from mandatory spending. Entitlements are certain government programs whereby the beneficiaries have a legally guaranteed right to the financial benefits, provided they meet certain eligibility criteria. Some entitlements are classified as mandatory spending, such as Social Security, Medicare and Medicaid, but others are classified as discretionary spending (e.g., veterans' benefits, unemployment, food stamps, and agricultural price supports). Likewise, some mandatory spending is not considered an entitlement (e.g., Congressional, White House and judicial salaries).

It's nearly impossible to accurately estimate the future cost of entitlement spending. Recipients are guaranteed the benefits provided they meet the eligibility requirements, and economic conditions have a significant impact on those who qualify. For example, a recession usually leads to higher unemployment, which means the payment of more unemployment benefits. Economists at the CBO and OMB are relatively accurate in estimating the cost of entitlements, but unexpected economic conditions can dramatically affect their estimates, both positively and negatively.

The cost of entitlements continues to escalate. Entitlement spending for FY 2015 consumed over 60% of the budget outlays. Social Security and Medicare constitute a large portion of entitlement spending. As more Baby Boomers retire in the next couple of decades, the cost of the current entitlement programs will devour an even larger portion of the budget, even if economic conditions improve dramatically.

It's exceptionally difficult to change entitlement programs. Understandably, the current recipients don't want their benefits reduced or eliminated and are motivated to make their voices heard. Aside from politicians' reluctance to upset their constituents, the internal organization of Congress makes entitlement reform difficult. Tension frequently exists between the congressional committees that write the laws governing the entitlement criteria and the budget and appropriations committees, which have to find ways to pay for them.

Members often request and are assigned to committees that are important to their constituents, and those members typically have a desire or feel a duty to maintain or expand the current programs. Consequently, it can be difficult to reconcile the aspiration to sustain existing entitlements with the ability to pay for them. Even if members of Congress support a reduction in overall spending, they want it to come from another program rather than the one they support. Politicking often results in members agreeing to larger across-the-board spending to prevent their own programs from being cut.

## Baseline Budgeting

Baseline budgeting is a process used to project future government expenditures. There are three primary principles that apply to baseline budgeting.

1. All current year spending is required and will continue indefinitely.
2. Current spending must be adjusted for inflation, cost of living adjustments, and population growth.
3. New programs are added to current spending, they are not a replacement.

Congress first started using baseline budgeting in 1974.[7] The essential rationale was to simplify the budgeting process. Rather than developing a budget from scratch each year, the current spending would serve as a floor for spending in the following fiscal year. Although current year spending is a great starting point, it's overly simplistic and fiscally irresponsible to assume all current spending is effective, efficient, and necessary for the next year.

The CBO and OMB develop the baseline budget from current legislation, but Congress does not have to accept the estimated spending of baseline budgeting. Any budget bill can override the baseline budget, but it's often politically difficult, especially for entitlements and mandatory spending. The result has been an ever-increasing level of federal spending.

The current baseline budgets estimate an annual increase in spending of 5-6%. By this methodology, spending automatically increases by 5-6% each year, even if Congress does nothing. Based on a 6% compounded rate (increase of 6% each year), a given expenditure more than doubles in 13 years. By simple mathematics, if the government spends $1 billion on a given program in 2015, it will spend more than $2 billion on the same program in 2028.

Baseline budgeting also factors into political discourse. In the eyes of Congress, the President, and many in Washington, spending cuts and increases are measured against the baseline. In their world, spending less than the baseline growth is deemed a cut, and an increase in spending only occurs if it exceeds the baseline amount. On this basis, the government can spend more than the previous year and still record a cut in spending.

If a particular item is budgeted for $100 in Fiscal 2014, the baseline increase for Fiscal 2015 is $6, to bring the total to $106. If the Fiscal 2015 budgeted amount is $105, it's classified as a $1 spending cut. In this way, politicians and pundits of all persuasions are able to claim they cut spending, even though the government actually spends more money each year.

## Baseline Budgeting

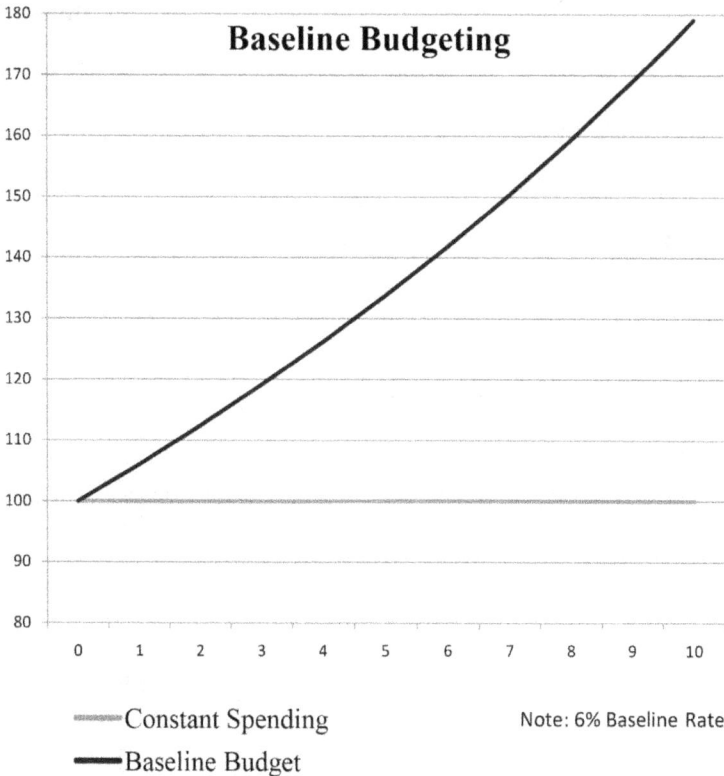

Constant Spending
Baseline Budget

Note: 6% Baseline Rate

## CBO Scoring

The CBO's role in the budget process is supposed to be objective and nonpartisan. Their stated purpose is to provide the necessary information to members of Congress to allow them to debate and decide policy.

The CBO's role is analogous to a scorekeeper in a basketball game. The scorekeeper's function is to add up the points based on the baskets made. Free throws count as one point, shots from a certain distance are two points, and baskets made from beyond an arc on the floor count as three. The scorekeeper didn't make the rules, nor do they decide whether the rules are fair or reasonable; they are simply objective parties who aren't involved in the game. Furthermore, basketball players don't get to create the rules or make the calls enforcing the rules. Those roles are reserved for referees and a sanctioning body (i.e., the NBA or NCAA).

Carrying the analogy to the federal budget, Congress acts as the players, referees and sanctioning body. When it comes to the CBO scoring of the federal budget, Congress sets and enforces the rules, while being active participants in the process. As a result, a scoring methodology which is supposed to be objective and free of partisan politics can easily be manipulated by Congress through the legislation they pass.

According to scoring guidelines, the CBO scores legislation based upon laws currently in existence. They ignore legislative history and the likelihood of future legislative changes. Although these principles are supposed to make the process more reliable, it can also misrepresent reality. The following are two such examples.

1. For years, legislation has existed that calls for a substantial reduction in the rate the federal government reimburses doctors to treat Medicare patients. There is a tremendous

36

risk that doctors will stop treating Medicare patients if their pay is dramatically decreased. Congress has repeatedly deferred the change in reimbursement rates. However, for CBO scoring purposes the savings are included in future budget projections because the legislation calls for the cuts to occur. When scoring the impact of the Affordable Care Act (AKA Obamacare), the CBO counted $500 billion in savings from reduced Medicare reimbursement to doctors. If history is a predictor of the future, these cuts will continue to be deferred, and the $500 billion savings will never materialize.

2. The Economic Growth and Tax Relief Reconciliation Act of 2001 and the Jobs and Growth Tax Relief Reconciliation Act of 2003 reduced tax rates for most taxpayers. Combined, these two laws were commonly referred to as the Bush tax cuts. In order to secure passage of the legislation, the lower tax rates were scheduled to expire at the end of 2010. Consequently, the CBO scoring process included increased tax revenue as of January 1, 2011, and any extension of the lower rates was scored as an expenditure adding to the deficit. When the rates were extended as part of the Tax Relief, Unemployment Insurance Reauth-orization, and Job Creation Act of 2010, the CBO scored the difference in actual versus projected

revenue for Fiscal 2011 as an expense, even though the revenue was essentially the same as Fiscal 2010.

These examples illustrate the problems with the CBO scoring process. Spending cuts which have never been made are counted as cost savings, and static revenues are counted as an expense. The CBO is not the problem, it's Congress. The CBO is simply the scorekeeper. Since Congress writes the legislation and the rules for the CBO to follow, they can manipulate the process in a manner that best suits their agenda.

## Justifying the Deficit

There are a myriad of justifications for U.S. government deficit spending. Politicians swiftly recite reasons why certain programs and expenditures are necessary. They may have noble motives and intentions, but they also have a vested interest in promoting government spending: they want to be re-elected. Voters tend to be happier when politicians direct federal spending towards their constituents. Everyone is generally supportive of cutting spending and the deficit, as long as the cuts affect someone else. A quote frequently attributed to former Speaker of the House, Tip O'Neill, summarizes this mentality: "All politics is local."

Aside from political motivations, there are legitimate economic reasons for governmental deficit spending. Part of Keynesian economic theory includes government spending during recessionary times. Even though government revenues may decline as a result of a recession (e.g., a reduction in tax receipts because individuals and businesses make less money), the government should not curtail expenditures. Keynesian economists believe a government should not try to balance its budget during these times. Instead, the government should increase spending on programs and public works projects to keep people employed and soften the recessionary impact. Keynesian economics was first embraced in the U.S. by President Franklin D. Roosevelt during the Great Depression and has been utilized, at least in part, by the U.S. government since the 1930s.

Economists and politicians also reference the size of the deficit in relationship to the U.S. Gross Domestic Product (GDP). They argue that continued deficit spending is acceptable, provided it remains below a certain percentage of the GDP. The premise is based upon the government's ability to service the debt. A certain level of GDP generates tax revenues, which the government can use to service the debt without going into default.

Despite all the economic and geopolitical challenges, U.S. GDP has increased every year since 1946, except for 2009. It's a testament to the strength and resiliency of the U.S. economy that it has continuously grown for nearly 70 years.

A growing economy has also helped to fund continuous deficit spending by the federal government. Table 3 illustrates the deficit as a percentage of GDP since 1934.

These justifications are reasonable and valid at a certain level, but they are all wrong and destructive when they become systemic and perpetual.

*Political Motivations.* In our modern political system, the ability to direct spending towards local people and projects is frequently a measure of a politician's effectiveness, and is important for re-election. Congress is also organized such that seniority equals influence, and more influence translates into increased power to direct federal spending. The result is a perverse, interrelated cycle. Members of Congress dole out money to help themselves get re-elected, and continual re-election gives them more power and influence to direct more spending.

You need only look at the number of pork barrel projects and special interest tax provisions that are slipped into unrelated legislation to recognize the political machinations that are part of everyday business in Washington. Few elected officials brazenly admit to such behavior, but incumbents will frequently tout their influence and seniority as a reason to be re-elected, especially when confronted with the prospect of losing their seats. Their ability to influence federal spending serves as an enticement for voters to re-elect them and keep the money flowing.

Politicians are elected to represent their constituents and do what is best for them. However, our representatives need to recognize situations in which the best interest of the nation is what's in the best interest of their constituents. Our elected officials should be willing to make unpopular decisions and risk losing the next election to do what's best for our country. Unfortunately, the long-term fiscal ramifications are often secondary to the short-term pressures of the next campaign cycle.

It is a perilous proposition when a primary focus of a democratic capitalistic government is the distribution of money to its constituents. As Alexis de Tocqueville said, "The American Republic will endure until the day Congress discovers that it can bribe the public with the public's money." The republic has not yet collapsed, but we are succumbing to the peril de Tocqueville foresaw. Our perpetual budget deficits and mounting national debt are clear indications that Congress is trying to buy us with our own money.

*Keynesian Economics.* Keynesian economics is a widely-accepted and legitimate theory of economics, even though there are opposing economic theories. Most economists acknowledge the role of government spending and monetary policy in stimulating the economy during recessionary periods, but there are credible questions about the efficiency and effectiveness of such spending. Aside from those issues, there is a fundamental flaw in Washington's embrace of Keynesian economics, which has two principles:

1. The government should spend money during recessionary periods to stimulate the economy.
2. The government should cut spending during times of prosperity.

Washington politicians have wholeheartedly embraced the premise of increased spending to stimulate the economy, but they have chosen to ignore the second principle. Rather than trim expenditures and pay back the debt borrowed to fund the stimulus spending, Congress and presidents have historically viewed the increased revenue as an opportunity to fund new projects and programs.

The lopsided embrace of Keynesian economics has resulted in the U.S. government posting only one year of surplus since 1960, not counting Social Security taxes. The inability to cut spending has produced perpetual deficits, which have increased exponentially over time. Increased spending creates a new floor for additional spending when the economy cycles through the next recession. This is how the deficit exploded to more than $1 trillion each year during Fiscal 2009-2012.

It may be a rather stark metaphor, but the United States has become addicted to spending and debt. Consider the symptoms and justifications of addictive behavior.

- We want to stop, but we can't.

- We know we need to stop, but we don't.

- The pangs of withdrawal seem so great, we won't stop.

- Short-term gratification overrides our long-term best interest.

- The longer we wait to stop, the harder and more painful it is to change.

Addicts didn't intend to succumb to the influence of their addiction, but they did. Similarly, the U.S. didn't intend to become addicted to debt, but it has.

If Washington wants to follow Keynesian economic theory, it must embrace both elements of the equation. It may be a good idea to increase spending during an economic downturn, but those spending increases must be temporary and curtailed once economic conditions improve. Without both, Keynesian economics becomes a political justification for increased spending, rather than the implementation of a complex macroeconomic policy.

*Deficit and GDP.* The calculation of the deficit to GDP percentage calculation is analogous to a lender evaluating your income to determine your qualification for a mortgage. For example, you typically can't qualify for a mortgage if your total loan payments exceed 30-35% of your annual income. Lenders recognize that you have other expenses beyond your mortgage. If your monthly payments consume too much of your income, the risk of default increases dramatically. With too much debt, it's unlikely you will be able to afford your living expenses and your monthly debt payments.

Under this premise, the more you earn, the more you can borrow. A person who makes $500,000 a year can more easily afford a $2,000 monthly mortgage payment than someone who makes $50,000. Therefore, the more you make the more you can afford to borrow.

Although GDP isn't the revenue of the federal government, it does impact federal revenues. As such, many economists postulate the government can afford annual deficits, provided they don't exceed 2-3% of GDP. The theory is similar to a home mortgage. The more revenues the U.S. government collects the more debt it can afford to service.

The theory is acceptable in the short-term, but long-term sustainability is dubious. Proponents of this proposition fail to acknowledge the effect of an ever-increasing debt load. Eventually the time arises when the cumulative effect of overspending becomes unaffordable.

The principle is not much different than your personal finances. Overspending by a small percentage of your annual income is not disastrous unless it continues unabated. Assume you make $100,000 per year and overspend by $3,000. How do you pay for your overspending? Either you take money from your savings, or you borrow it. If you don't have any savings (which the U.S. government doesn't have), you borrow, with the promise to repay someday. The debt service on $3,000 is probably a couple hundred dollars a year, which is entirely affordable. This overspending and borrowing doesn't affect your financial situation unless it keeps going for years, or decades.

If you continue to fund your overspending by borrowing, the debt service will continue to consume a larger portion of your income. Even if your income rises, the borrowing costs will escalate and become unaffordable. This exactly how people get into trouble with credit cards and consumer debt. The low monthly payments are easily affordable at the beginning, but a pattern of overspending funded by borrowing money eventually leads to a financial crisis.

The U.S. government is not much different from an individual in this example, except it has overspent consistently for the past 80 years. The overspending was small in some years, but ballooned to 25-30% of revenues during the Great Recession of 2008-2009. As a result, a larger portion of annual revenues are being consumed to pay the interest—forget about paying down the $18 trillion principal.

The supposition that there is little economic concern for annual budget deficits which don't exceed 2-3% of GDP is true for a short period of time. However, the belief that continuous and perpetual annual deficits are economically viable is illogical, irrational and simply unsustainable. No individual, family, business or *government* can overspend forever.

Summary

You don't have to be a financial wizard to understand that the federal government has a spending problem. Just consider two simple facts: the government has overspent for 55 of the last 56 years, and all federal taxes, fees and revenue sources would have to increase by nearly 20% in fiscal 2016 to balance the budget. Common sense tells you this is a problem.

Just like dealing with your personal finances, reducing spending is hard and painful, but often necessary. The longer you wait the more commitments you make, and the more accustomed you become to living in a certain manner. Waiting rarely eliminates the pain; it only prolongs it, and usually magnifies it.

Annual budget deficits are a problem, but this is not the sole problem facing our great nation. Not only do we have to deal with annual budget deficits, we also need to contend with the debt.

# CHAPTER 3
# THE U.S. DEBT

~~~~~~

## Overview

The cumulative amount of money borrowed by the U.S. Treasury and other government agencies to fund the operations and expenditures of the U.S. government is the national debt. This debt total represents the cumulative borrowing through a specific date. As of December 31, 2015, the U.S. debt was approximately $18.922 trillion, and increasing by more than $1.5 billion each day. You can go to www.usdebtclock.org for an updated tally.

The U.S. debt is allocated into two primary categories based upon who lent the money. The public debt is held by investors, which includes individuals, business entities, financial institutions, the Federal Reserve, and state, local, and foreign governments. As of December 31, 2015, $13.672 trillion (72.3%) of the total debt is owed to the public. The remaining $5.250 trillion is intragovernmental debt.[8] This portion of the debt constitutes money owed to other governmental agencies and programs. Intragovernmental debt is not traded and is essentially an IOU from one agency or department of the federal government to another.

**Federal Debt**

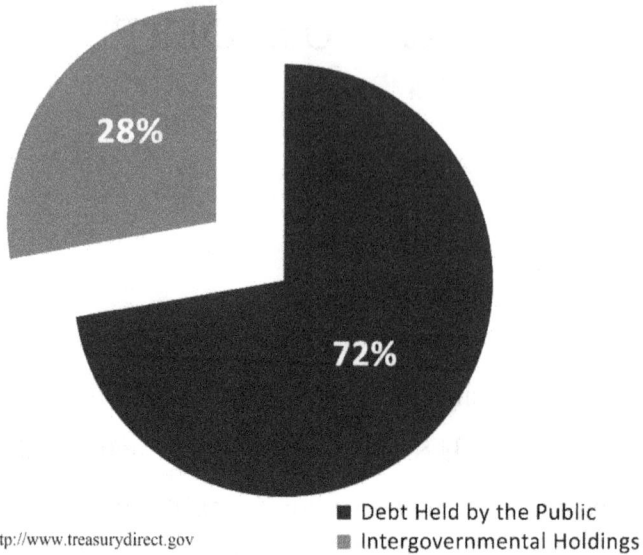

28%

72%

Source: http://www.treasurydirect.gov

■ Debt Held by the Public
■ Intergovernmental Holdings

## Millions, Billions and Trillions

It's easy to get lost in all the -illions, especially since they sound the same. However, the value differential is exponential. By simple math, a billion is 1,000 million and a trillion is 1,000 billion. Thus, a trillion is a million millions: that's 12 zeros.

Even though most of us will never be millionaires, we can at least comprehend $1 million. A billion dollars is a lot harder to comprehend, but there are a few billionaires in the world. It may be hard to fathom what it would be like to have a billion dollars, but we can name people who have that amount of money (Bill Gates, Warren Buffet, Larry Ellison, and Mark Zuckerberg, to name just a few). It's nearly impossible to fully grasp what $1 trillion represents. There are no trillionaires in the world, and no one is even close. Bill Gates is currently the wealthiest person in the world, and is only about 5% of the way to having a trillion dollars.

Consider the following differences between one million and one trillion. A U.S. $1 bill is 6.1 inches long.

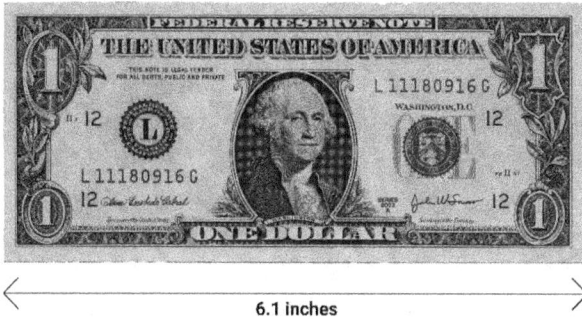

6.1 inches

If you laid one million $1 dollar bills end to end, they would stretch for 6,100,000 inches. There are 63,360 inches in a mile. Thus, $1 million would cover a distance of 96.27 miles, which is approximately the distance between Los Angeles and Santa Barbara, California.

One billion dollars would reach 96,275 miles. The distance around the earth's equator is approximately 24,900 miles, which means $1 billion dollars would circle the earth 3.9 times.

One trillion dollars would stretch 96,275,000 miles. The average distance between the earth and the sun is 93 million miles, and the circumference of the sun is estimated to be 2.7 million miles. Therefore, one trillion dollar bills laid end to end would stretch from the earth around the sun, and start heading back to earth again.

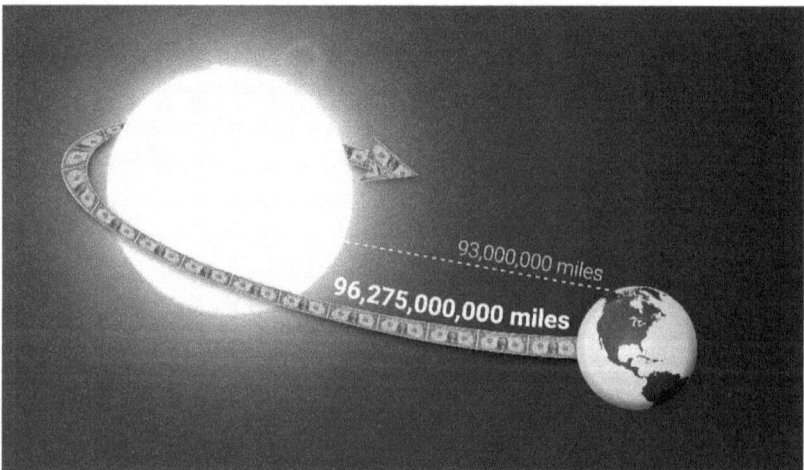

Using the illustration of laying $1 bills end-to-end, our $18 trillion debt would encircle the sun and the earth more than nine times. It's virtually incomprehensible.

## Intragovernmental Debt

Nearly two-thirds of the intragovernmental debt is held by the Social Security Trust. For the past few decades, the amount of Social Security taxes collected from workers exceeded the amount of money needed to pay the requisite Social Security benefits. The surplus money was loaned from the Social Security Trust to the U.S. Treasury and spent by the various agencies and departments of the U.S. government. The chapter on Social Security will provide a greater analysis of intragovernmental debt and the implications for the total debt, annual deficits and the future of Social Security.

As previously stated, the intragovernmental debt is not a traded security. In effect, the Federal government has borrowed money from itself. The intragovernmental debt has political, public policy and long-term budgetary implications, but in real economic terms, it's nothing more than an accounting entry by the federal government.

## Public Debt

The U.S. Treasury borrows money from public investors by selling various debt securities. Treasury bills have a maturity date no more than one year from the date of issue. Treasury notes have a maturity date of at least one year, but fewer than ten years. Treasury bonds carry a maturity date greater than ten years from the date of issue.

With a few exceptions, interest rates are determined at the date of issue and are fixed for the duration of the security.

Treasury securities are initially sold via a public auction. Investors can purchase bills, notes and bonds directly from the U.S. Treasury, or they can purchase them through an investment firm. Although each Treasury security has a defined maturity date, an investor is not required to hold the security until it matures. Treasury securities are freely traded on the public bond markets. The trading price is usually different from the stated value of the security based upon the differential between the current interest rate and the stated interest rate. For example, a $10,000 treasury bond with a 5% interest rate will usually trade for more than $10,000 if current interest rate is less than 5% and will trade for less than $10,000 if the current rate rises above 5%.

As interest rates have fallen over the past few years, the Treasury has systematically extended the average maturity of the U.S. public debt. The following chart produced by the Treasury Department shows the average maturity of U.S. Treasury securities from 1980 to mid-2012.

# Longer-Term Treasury Debt Portfolio

**Weighted average maturity of marketable
U.S. Treasury securities outstanding months**

MONTHS

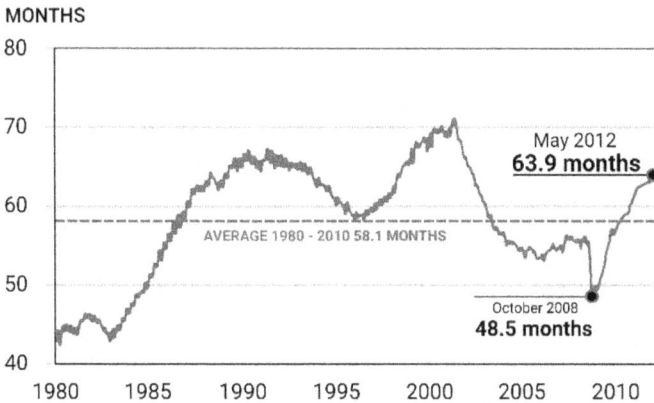

May 2012
**63.9 months**

AVERAGE 1980 - 2010 58.1 MONTHS

October 2008
**48.5 months**

Source: Treasury                    **U.S. Department of the Treasury**

As the chart illustrates, the average maturity has increased from 48.5 months in October 2008 to 63.9 months in May 2012. Provided interest rates remain low, the Treasury will likely continue to extend the average maturity of public debt.

With historically low interest rates, extending the maturity is a good financial strategy and will benefit future U.S. taxpayers. It's like refinancing your home mortgage at a lower rate; a lower interest rate will save you thousands of dollars over the term of the loan. Extending the average maturity rate of Treasury securities by locking in historically low interest rates for many years to come should save U.S. taxpayers billions of dollars. While this is an excellent short-term strategy, there are inherent long-term risks, which will be discussed in the section on interest rates.

Public Investors

The U.S. Federal Reserve Bank (AKA the Fed) is the largest owner of public debt. On December 31, 2015 the Fed held $2.462 trillion of U.S. Treasury bills, notes and bonds.[9] Thus, the Fed owned approximately 13 % of the total $18.922 trillion debt, and 18% of the $13.672 trillion public debt.

Created by Congress in 1913, the Federal Reserve System is not an agency of the U.S. government because Congress wanted the Fed to be insulated from political pressure in developing monetary policy. Instead, the Fed is a governmental entity managed by a Board of Governors who are nominated by the President and confirmed by the Senate. The Fed's two primary responsibilities are setting U.S. monetary policy and regulating banking activity.

The involvement of the President and Senate adds a political dynamic to the Fed. Unlike other departments and agencies, the Fed doesn't report to the President, nor does it depend upon Congress for funding. The relationship is akin to the federal judiciary: members of the Board of Governors are nominated by the President and confirmed by the Senate, but once confirmed, the Governors are free to act in their best judgment, despite the opinions of the President or Congress. Unlike federal judges, the Fed Governors have term limits.

Since the Fed is not classified as a government agency, its holdings of U.S. Treasuries are not considered intragovernmental debt. Furthermore, the Fed buys and sells its Treasury holdings on the open market, whereas the intragovernmental debt is only issued between the Treasury and a specified federal agency.

Beyond the Fed, foreign governments are the largest investors in U.S. Treasuries. There has been a lot of political discussion over the amount of debt owed to China. Although China is the largest holder of public debt, it barely exceeds the debt held by Japan. Both countries held more than $1 trillion of U.S. debt as of December 31, 2015, with China holding $124 billion more than Japan. See the chart below for the top 10 foreign holders of public debt.[10]

### Foreign Holders of U.S. Debt as of December 31, 2015

|  | Millions | Percentage of Public Debt |
|---|---|---|
| China | 1,246.1 | 9.11% |
| Japan | 1,122.6 | 8.21% |
| Ireland | 265.1 | 1.94% |
| Brazil | 254.8 | 1.86% |
| United Kingdom | 218.3 | 1.60% |
| Switzerland | 231.9 | 1.70% |
| Luxembourg | 200.5 | 1.47% |
| Hong Kong | 200.2 | 1.46% |
| Taiwan | 178.7 | 1.31% |
| Belgium | 121.7 | 0.89% |
| India | 116.8 | 0.85% |

Source: http://Department of the Treasury/Federal Reserve Board

Some political rhetoric suggests China is financing the current budget deficits. The Fiscal 2015 deficit was more than $438 billion, and China's total investment in U.S. debt is $1.246 trillion. China has held more than $1 trillion of U.S. Treasury securities for years. Since their holdings have been relatively constant, they can't be funding a majority of the deficit spending by the Federal government.

## Contingent Obligations

Contingent obligations are liabilities which are dependent upon some future event, and the obligation to pay is uncertain. Debt guarantees are a contingent liability. Provided the borrower pays the debt in full, there is no obligation on behalf of the guarantor to pay any money. However, if the borrower defaults, the guarantor can be forced to pay a portion, or the entire amount owed.

You may have created a contingent liability the first time you financed a car or house. Depending on your income or credit history, the bank may have required someone to co-sign the loan. The co-signer's guarantee was classified as a contingent liability. Provided you made all of the payments on time, it didn't cost the co-signer anything. If for some reason you stopped making payments, the lender would pursue the co-signer for the money owed. The co-signer's obligation to pay was contingent on your failure to pay, which presumably was not expected at the time the loan was signed.

The $18 trillion national debt only includes the direct obligation issued by the U.S. Treasury. It does not include any contingent liabilities, such as home mortgages and student loans; these represent the largest contingent obligations of the U.S. government. As of December 31, 2015, there were approximately $13.8 trillion of mortgages and $1.3 trillion of student loans,[11] of which most have been guaranteed by the U.S. government.

In an attempt to increase home ownership and make higher education more affordable, Congress created government-sponsored enterprises (GSE) to underwrite home mortgages and student loans. There are multiple GSEs that issue debt securities. Since the late 1960s, only mortgages offered by Ginnie Mae are explicitly backed by the full faith and credit of the U.S. government. Although not carrying an explicit guarantee, debt securities issued by the other GSEs carry an "implicit guarantee" of the U.S. government.

These guarantees cost the government nothing, unless homeowners or former students fail to pay their debts. While it seems rather unlikely that this would happen to any large extent in America, you only need to consider the number of homes which have been subject to default and foreclosure since 2008. During the height of the financial crisis, the U.S. government took Fannie Mae and Freddie Mac under conservatorship. The implicit guarantee of the U.S. government was certainly a factor in the government's decision to take this action, rather than allowing these entities to go bankrupt. The U.S. Treasury had to transfer $187.5 billion to keep these entities afloat and reimburse investors who lost money when thousands of homeowners defaulted.[12]

Under the original terms of the bailout, the Treasury was supposed to receive a 10% preferred rate of return on the money lent to Fannie Mae and Freddie Mac. However, William Isaac, the former Inspector General of the Federal Housing Finance Agency (FHFA), described a change the U.S. Treasury implemented in 2012.[13] As explained by Mr.

Isaac, the Treasury has been taking 100% of Fannie and Freddie's profits over the previous few years as a 100% dividend, and plans to continue this practice for the foreseeable future. Since this practice has returned $227 billion to the government coffers, it appears the bailout was a good investment by the federal government.

Mr. Isaac's explanation exposed the potential danger of this practice. By not allowing Fannie or Freddie to accumulate capital through its profits, neither entity will have the capital reserves required to withstand another significant downturn in the housing market. The bailout in 2008 was necessitated by Fannie and Freddie depleting its capital from mortgage defaults; if Fannie and Freddie have minimal capital, the need for government funds will be required even sooner.

As contingent liabilities, it is not appropriate to count the entire $14 trillion of GSE loans as a liability of the U.S. government, but it's also unwise to ignore the entire amount. Since history has proven the U.S. taxpayer can be on the hook for defaulted mortgages, some portion of the GSE mortgages and student loans should be treated as a contingent liability and included as part of the total debt owed by the U.S. government.

## Interest Rates

During Fiscal 2015, the U.S. government paid $402.4 billion in interest on its debt. The average outstanding debt during 2015 was approximately $17.99 trillion, resulting in an average interest rate of 2.24%. The following chart shows the outstanding debt at the end of each fiscal year since 2000, and the interest paid by the U.S.

government over the past 15 years. It also shows the average interest rate paid on the outstanding Treasury debt during the same period.

### AVERAGE INTEREST RATE
### U.S. DEBT
### 2000-2015

|  | Outstanding Debt (millions) | Total Interest (millions) | Average Interest Rate |
|---|---|---|---|
| September 30, 2015 | 18,150,618 | 402,435 | 2.24% |
| September 30, 2014 | 17,824,071 | 430,812 | 2.49% |
| September 30, 2013 | 16,738,184 | 415,689 | 2.53% |
| September 30, 2012 | 16,066,241 | 359,796 | 2.33% |
| September 30, 2011 | 14,790,340 | 454,393 | 3.21% |
| September 30, 2010 | 13,561,623 | 413,955 | 3.25% |
| September 30, 2009 | 11,909,829 | 383,071 | 3.49% |
| September 30, 2008 | 10,024,725 | 451,154 | 4.74% |
| September 30, 2007 | 9,007,653 | 429,978 | 4.91% |
| September 30, 2006 | 8,506,974 | 405,872 | 4.94% |
| September 30, 2005 | 7,932,710 | 352,350 | 4.60% |
| September 30, 2004 | 7,379,053 | 321,566 | 4.54% |
| September 30, 2003 | 6,783,231 | 318,149 | 4.89% |
| September 30, 2002 | 6,228,236 | 332,537 | 5.53% |
| September 30, 2001 | 5,807,463 | 359,508 | 6.26% |
| September 30, 2000 | 5,674,178 | 361,998 | 6.39% |

Source: http://www.treasurydirect.gov

As previously mentioned, the Treasury has made a concerted effort to extend the average maturity of outstanding Treasury obligations, primarily to save U.S. taxpayers money by taking advantage of historically low interest rates. Taxpayers are already benefiting from this strategy. The interest paid in Fiscal 2015 was approximately the same as paid in Fiscal 2006, even though the total debt more than doubled over the past nine years. The average interest rate steadily declined from 2008 through 2012, and has basically been flat for the past four years.

Extending the average maturity of the outstanding debt and taking advantage of historically low interest rates is financially prudent and has great benefits. . . for the short term. However, there is an ominous problem lurking on the horizon. It's unlikely the current rates will remain this low forever. For a variety of reasons, the cost of borrowing money will eventually rise. After bottoming out in 2012, interest rates have been creeping upward. As illustrated, this is also causing the cost of borrowing by the federal government to rise as well, albeit very slowly.

Imagine what will happen if interest rates bounce back to pre-2008 rates. If average interest rates were to escalate to 5%, the interest cost on the outstanding debt would skyrocket. At a rate of 5%, the interest expense on $18 trillion of debt is $900 billion each year. Keep in mind, the Treasury collected $3.25 trillion in revenue in Fiscal 2015. Thus, interest on the national debt could easily consume nearly one-third of all money coming into the federal coffers. The CBO projects the deficits from fiscal 2014 through 2020 will add another $3.775 trillion to the debt; this will push total debt near $21 trillion. At a rate of 5%, the annual interest cost on $21 trillion would be $1.05 trillion.

Although there are clear differences between a home mortgage and the national debt, a comparison can be made. The current financing of the national debt could be considered analogous to homeowners who purchased homes with subprime mortgages, which were a significant contributor to the collapse of the U.S. housing market in 2007 and 2008. A subprime mortgage carried a low introductory interest rate, but at a certain point in the mortgage term the interest rates increased. This rate change significantly increased the monthly payment, and for many borrowers it was more than they could afford. Many defaulted soon after the rate increase took effect.

The U.S. debt is not a subprime mortgage, but all of the current U.S. debt will effectively be refinanced at some future date. As depicted in Illustration 10, the average maturity of all Treasury securities is 63.9 months (just more than five years). None of the budget plans proposed by the President, House or Senate project a balanced budget within the next 10 years. Thus, for the next decade, the national debt will continue to grow and none of the current debt will get paid off. This essentially means all of the current debt will mature and new Treasury securities will need to be sold at the prevailing interest rate. The Treasury may be able to issue notes in 2015 with an interest rate of 2-3%, but five years from that point the interest rate could be much higher. The Treasury is currently reaping the benefit of swapping higher interest rate obligations for lower rates ones, but eventually the reverse will happen: lower interest rate securities will mature and their replacements will carry a higher rate of interest.

An average interest rate of 5% is not unreasonable or unrealistic. Although interest rates fluctuated throughout the 1980s, 1990s and mid-2000s, the interest rate on Treasury securities hovered around 5%.

There were economic booms and recessions, but interest rates didn't reach double digits as they did in the late 1970s. Therefore, it's completely reasonable to expect interest rates to climb in the coming years. Prior to 2008, Treasury rates near 5% were considered to be somewhat normal, but there is no guaranteed ceiling on interest rates. Any rate increase will be hard to manage, but the higher the rate, the more devastating the impact will be.

Low interest rates are presently saving us money, but they are also disguising the potential long-term cost of our national debt. Unless Congress and the President make significant progress in balancing the budget, the national debt will continue to climb and the interest cost of carrying the debt could increase exponentially. Absent meaningful budgetary reforms, the ballooning debt and skyrocketing interest expense will consume an increasingly larger portion of federal revenues.

Bond Rating

The highest rating any bond can receive from Fitch Ratings and Standard & Poor's is AAA, and Aaa from Moody's. Since the inception of bond ratings, U.S. Treasury securities carried the AAA/Aaa from all three agencies, until August 5, 2011. Days after the protracted debate over raising the debt ceiling and spending cuts concluded with the passage of the Budget Control Act of 2011, Standard & Poor's dropped its rating one notch, from AAA to AA+. The ratings change was also coupled with a negative outlook on U.S. Treasuries. Although Fitch Ratings and Moody's have yet to downgrade their ratings, both agencies identified U.S. Treasuries as having a negative outlook.

## LONG TERM BOND RATINGS

| Category | Moody's | S&P | Fitch |
|---|---|---|---|
| Prime | Aaa | AAA | AAA |
| High Grade | Aa1 | AA+ | AA+ |
| | Aa2 | AA | AA |
| | Aa3 | AA- | AA- |
| Upper Medium Grade | A1 | A+ | A+ |
| | A2 | A | A |
| | A3 | A- | A- |
| Lower Medium Grade | Baa1 | BBB+ | BBB+ |
| | Baa2 | BBB | BBB |
| | Baa3 | BBB- | BBB- |
| Non Investment Grade | Ba1 | BB+ | BB+ |
| | Ba2 | BB | BB |
| | Ba3 | BB- | BB- |
| Highly Speculative | B1 | B+ | B+ |
| | B2 | B | B |
| | B3 | B- | B- |
| Substantial Risks | Caa1 | CCC+ | |
| Extremely Speculative | Caa2 | CCC | CCC |
| In Default with Little | Caa3 | CCC- | |
| Prospect for Recovery | Ca | CC | |

The drop in the Standard & Poor's rating was rather negligible, but it sparked a melee of political finger-pointing. For decades, U.S. Treasuries were effectively viewed as the gold standard against which all other securities were measured. The idea that other nations had a bond rating higher than the U.S. was a blow to American pride and prompted a lot of blame tossed around Washington. It was also an indication of trouble in paradise, and an early warning sign from a nonpolitical entity that the U.S. deficits and debt might be getting out of control.

In the end, other than damaging the psyche and pride of America, the Standard & Poor's ratings decrease had no real impact on the U.S. Treasury market. In fact, Treasury prices rose and interest rates declined in the weeks following the downgrade. However, this impact may only be temporary, and was likely a reflection of other market factors, such as concerns regarding the European sovereign debt crisis.

A bond rating has no direct influence over the interest rate, pricing, or trading of any bond. The ratings are simply intended to help investors make an informed decision about the credit worthiness of an investment. A sovereign bond rating is an assessment of a country's ability to repay its debts, which includes economic and political factors. In reality, there is very little risk that a country will default on its debts. Since virtually every nation has the ability to print its own currency, it will simply print more money to pay off the debt. Thus, the risk is effectively not whether an investor will get paid, but what their payment will be worth. Even countries that are part of a common currency, like the Euro, can choose to exit the common currency and form their own currency. For example, throughout much of 2012 and again in 2015, there was great speculation and concern that Greece would exit the Euro and would revert to the drachma.

The ratings downgrade may have had little short-term effect, but the long-term impact may be profound. If the debt and deficit outlook for the U.S. doesn't change significantly in the future, investors could have a less favorable view of the creditworthiness of the U.S. government, which will affect interest rates and bond prices. When investors have a less favorable outlook on U.S. debt, they will demand a higher interest rate to continue purchasing U.S. bonds. As a result, the Treasury will have no choice but to increase bond rates in order to attract the necessary investors to keep the country solvent. The increased interest cost will put more pressure on the current deficit and debt.

## Summary

The size of the national debt is daunting. However, owing nearly $19 trillion in debt is not the biggest problem; of greater concern is the rate at which the debt is growing. The national debt has doubled in fewer than eight years, and has grown by more than 20% in the past five. The CBO expects the total debt to exceed $21 trillion by 2020, and based on current policies, the U.S. will continue over spending and borrowing for decades.

There is little good news about the U.S. national debt. Probably the most positive aspect of the debt is that over 40% is essentially held by the U.S. government. The Social Security Trust Fund and other federal agencies hold $5.25 trillion and the Federal Reserve Bank holds $2.4 trillion. However, this silver lining will soon lose some of its luster. For years, excess Social Security taxes have helped fund government overspending, but that is due to change soon. For the next few decades, the debt challenges of the United States are going to be exacerbated by the commitments of Social Security.

# CHAPTER 4
# SOCIAL SECURITY

Overview

It may seem inappropriate to include Social Security in a book dedicated to the deficit and the debt. According to many politicians and government reports, Social Security is stable and secure. They acknowledge potential long-term solvency issues, but downplay any immediate concerns.

As stated in the previous chapter, Social Security currently has nearly $3 trillion in assets, at least according to the government's accounting records. The defenders of the status quo often cite this fact to deflect criticism from the proponents of change.

Hopefully there is one thing you've learned by reading this book, or may have already known: the reality of national political and economic issues is usually different from what politicians and pundits say. Our politicians have become master illusionists. An illusionist keeps you focused on one thing to draw your attention away from what's happening elsewhere.

In technical terms, Social Security is a governmental trust whose assets, income and expenses are kept separate from the other operations of the U.S. government. As depicted in Table 1, trust funds are accounted for separately from the other operations of the federal government.

The section below on the Social Security lockbox will explain the reality of this separate accounting. For now, think in these terms: a married couple may have 'my money,' 'your money,' and 'our money.' This segregation may be great for tracking money, paying bills, and making financial decisions, but at the end of the day, as a married couple it's all 'our money.' Furthermore, the decisions and actions of one spouse eventually affect the other, and the family as a whole.

This same symbiotic relationship exists between Social Security and the rest of the federal government. While many act as though they are completely separate and unrelated, this section will reveal their connection, and future fiscal impact.

History and Background

Social Security was passed in 1935 as part of President Franklin D. Roosevelt's New Deal. From its inception, Social Security was intended to provide assistance to the elderly. In the depths of the Great Depression, most seniors had lost their retirement savings through the stock market crash and bank failures. The lack of personal savings and a pension plan, along with rampant unemployment, left a majority of seniors impoverished.

Social Security was designed to provide seniors with a modest retirement pension and a small death benefit to help families pay funeral costs for deceased family members. Beyond taking care of seniors' basic needs, there was an ancillary motive behind Social Security: reducing unemployment. Without a pension or adequate savings, older Americans couldn't retire and needed to continue working, provided they could find a job. A guaranteed monthly retirement benefit gave aging Americans an incentive to leave their jobs, which would presumably be filled by younger unemployed people.

Social Security may not have dramatically reduced the U.S. unemployment rate during the Great Depression, but it provided an enticement for older Americans to retire. Social Security benefits may not fund a lavish retirement, or be the reason most seniors retire, but a majority of Americans would be reluctant to retire without their Social Security benefits.

## Early Amendments

Social Security payroll taxes were first collected in 1937, which was the same year lump-sum death benefits commenced. Monthly retirement benefit payments started in January 1940. Congress made a variety of amendments to Social Security in 1939, including the following:

- A trust fund was established to hold any excess taxes collected over the benefits paid,
- Benefits for spouses and children were increased,
- The lump-sum death benefit was eliminated, and

- Social Security taxation became part of the Internal Revenue Code administered by the IRS and was renamed the Federal Insurance Contribution Act (i.e., FICA taxes).

## Program Expansion

Disability benefits were added in 1956, coupled with a tax rate increase to 4.0% (2.0% for the employee and 2.0% for the employer). As part of President Lyndon Johnson's Great Society program, Medicare and Medicaid were added by the Social Security Act of 1965. Medicare provides medical coverage to people over age 65 who also qualify for Social Security retirement or disability benefits. Medicaid provides medical coverage to qualified low-income individuals and families. Medicaid is funded jointly by federal and state governments and is administered by the individual states.

In 1972, Congress approved a one-time 20% increase in Social Security benefits, and added an automatic cost-of-living adjustment (COLA) to future benefits. Although they intended benefits to increase at the rate of inflation, a technical mistake caused the benefits to increase at twice the rate of inflation. The prolonged recession of the 1970s included double-digit inflation. Combined with the double-indexing of Social Security benefits, Social Security's financial position quickly eroded from cash surpluses to financial crisis. In 1977, Congress passed legislation to fix the double-indexing mistake. They also increased the tax rate from 4% to 12.3% (6.15% for the employee and 6.15% for the employer). These corrections were intended to fix the system until 2030.

Solvency Crisis

Although the 1977 Social Security amendments were supposed to make Social Security solvent for the next 53 years, another crisis erupted a few years later. By 1982, some projections indicated the Social Security Trust Fund would be depleted by 1983, and there was speculation certain benefits would be curtailed.

In 1981, President Ronald Reagan and Congress established the National Commission on Social Security Reform. Since it was headed by Alan Greenspan, the group became known as the Greenspan Commission. The task of the Greenspan Commission was to study and make recommendations regarding the short-term financial crisis facing Social Security. The Greenspan Commission issued its report in January 1983 and their findings became the basis for the 1983 amendments, which include:

- Delaying the cost-of-living adjustments from July to January of each year,
- Subjecting up to one-half of Social Security benefits to income taxation,
- Accelerating previously passed Social Security and Medicare tax increases,
- Requiring newly-hired federal employees to participate in Social Security, and
- Raising the retirement age starting in 2009.[14]

The 1983 amendments were the last significant changes to Social Security and Medicare. These changes were intended to generate substantial surpluses in the Social Security Trust Fund which would cover the benefits of the Baby Boomers, who were expected to start retiring early in the 21st century.

Current Status

In the past 30 years, there have been minor tweaks but no meaningful changes to Social Security benefits or taxes. The lack of legislative changes is not a confirmation that Social Security is on firm financial footing; instead, it's more reflective of the political climate in Washington and the reluctance to alter promises made to Social Security beneficiaries. The situation may be not as dire as it was in the early 1980s, but there are legitimate short-term and long-term concerns regarding Social Security.

The Social Security Administration is an independent agency headed by the Social Security Commissioner. Social Security money and programs are divided into three different trust funds overseen by an identical Board of Trustees composed of three Cabinet Secretaries, the Social Security Commissioner, and two other individuals. The Trustees issue an annual report summarizing the current financial status of Social Security. Below are a few highlights of the report issued on July 22, 2015.[15]

- Social Security provides benefits to 59 million people, and 166 million people paid Social Security payroll taxes.
- The Social Security Trust Fund reports assets of $2.789 trillion.

- Total 2014 revenues were $884 billion ($786 billion of taxes and $98 billion of interest on Trust Fund assets), and $859 billion of benefits were paid.

- Benefits exceeded tax revenues by $73 billion, and the benefits are expected to exceed tax revenues by $68 billion in 2016.

- The current surplus is a result of a $98 billion interest payment from the U.S. Treasury's general fund for the $2.789 trillion lent by Social Security to fund general government operations.

- The Trust Fund has $60 billion of reserves left to pay disability claims, and the Disability Insurance Trust reserves are expected to be depleted by October, 2016.

- Total revenues are expected to exceed benefit payments from 2015-2021, which includes the interest earned on the excess assets lent to the Treasury to fund other government operations.

- After 2021, benefits will continue to exceed tax revenues and interest collected on the intragovernmental debt (i.e., Social Security will start tapping the Trust Fund assets to pay benefits).

- By 2035 all of the Trust Fund reserves will be depleted.

- The unfunded benefits for the next 75 years are estimated to be $10.7 trillion.

Social Security may not be in crisis at the moment, but the above facts indicate that the long-term sustainability of Social Security in its current form is highly doubtful. While some of the most ardent supporters of the current program argue there is nothing to be concerned about, the demographics of the nation and our financial condition do not bode well for the current programs to continue without modification.

Worker Ratio

Since its inception, Social Security was designed as a pay-go system. Taxes collected by current workers were supposed to cover the benefits paid. The pay-go structure has led some critics to refer to Social Security as a Ponzi scheme (an illegal investment scheme where current investors' money is used to pay previous investors). A pay-go system is not an illegal Ponzi scheme, but it is different from most pension plans which require employers and employees to set aside money to pay future benefits.

Given the tax rates assessed against working individuals, the pay-go system only works when there are more workers than beneficiaries. This worked extremely well during the early years of Social Security, but the ratio of workers to beneficiaries has dramatically diminished over the past 70 years.

# SOCIAL SECURITY WORKER RATIO

| Year | Covered Workers (thousands) | Beneficiaries (thousands) | Ratio |
|------|------|------|------|
| 1940 | 35,390 | 222 | 159.4 |
| 1950 | 48,280 | 2,930 | 16.5 |
| 1960 | 72,530 | 14,262 | 5.1 |
| 1980 | 113,656 | 35,118 | 3.2 |
| 2000 | 155,295 | 46,176 | 3.4 |
| 2010 | 156,725 | 53,398 | 2.9 |

Source: http://Social Security online - History

According to the 2015 Trustee's Report, there were 165.6 million workers and 58.6 million beneficiaries, representing a ratio of 2.8. As the table above depicts, the ratio of workers to beneficiaries has steadily declined over the past 70 years. Current demographics of the U.S. population will cause this ratio to shrink even further over the next 20 years.

Approximately 76 million children (the Baby Boomers) were born between 1946 and 1965.[16] The eldest Baby Boomers turned 65 in 2010, and they will continue to swell the ranks of the U.S. population over age 65 for the next two decades. The U.S. Census Bureau projects the percentage of population over 65 will increase from 13% in 2010 to more than 19% in 2030. Virtually all of them expect to draw money from Social Security. As a result, the Social Security Administration expects the worker/beneficiary ratio to drop to 2.2:1 by 2030.

In 2015, the average Social Security recipient received approximately $14,800 in annual benefits, and each worker contributed $3,900. By 2025, the worker ratio is projected to drop to 2.4:1 and each beneficiary is projected to receive more than $20,000 in Social Security benefits. With a worker to beneficiary ratio of 2.4:1, each worker will have to contribute more than $8,300 to fully pay the benefits to Social Security recipients in 2025. Thus, under a pay-go system, Social Security taxes would have to more than double in the next ten years to collect sufficient taxes to pay the required benefits.

Recognizing the demographic challenges of the Baby Boom generation, Congress created a deviation from the pay-go system as part of the 1983 amendments. Their solution was to accelerate a planned increase in Social Security and Medicare taxes to build up a reserve of assets that could be drawn upon in future years to pay benefits to the Baby Boomers. The increased taxes of the late 1900s and early 2000s were supposed to create a surplus of assets to draw upon for future benefits. It worked. The cumulative surpluses have produced an excess of $2.7 trillion in taxes, which constitute the assets held by the Social Security Trust Fund.

## Social Security Trust Fund

The Social Security Trust Fund is the only thing preventing the entire Social Security system from being classified as insolvent and facing a major crisis. A difficult question for the American public to ask is: Does the Social Security Trust Fund exist? The answer is yes . . . and no. A contradiction? Not surprising, given the political issues and posturing surrounding Social Security.

Virtually every elected official in Washington adamantly insists the Social Security Trust Fund exists. In some respects, they are absolutely correct. The Social Security Trust Fund holds $2.7 trillion of intragovernmental debt (see the discussion in the previous chapter). The only assets held by the Social Security Trust Fund are these special IOUs from the U.S. Treasury. Thus, according to the budgetary laws written by Congress, the Social Security Trust Fund has $2.7 trillion of assets, and based on the law, every person and report citing this fact is correct.

However, go back to the analogy at the beginning of this chapter involving a married couple managing their finances using my money, your money and our money. Consider this example: the wife makes more money than she spends on an annual basis. To help prepare for her future retirement, each year she transfers her excess funds to her husband in exchange for an IOU from him. On paper, each IOU is classified as an asset, so she believes she is saving for her future retirement. After three decades of transferring money and receiving IOUs from her husband, she has a sizeable nest egg saved to fund her retirement.

However, rather than using his wife's money to purchase bonds, stocks or real estate, the husband spent most of her money each year. It wasn't necessarily all frivolous spending; he paid medical bills for the family, tuition bills for their children, and gave a lot of it away to help those in need. Even though his spending may have been necessary, or for a good cause, the bottom line is that virtually all the money his wife invested with him is gone. With no real asset reserve to draw upon, how does he repay the IOUs to his wife when she needs the money for retirement? No matter how they tracked it on paper, his overspending put their collective retirement at risk.

This analogy essentially describes the situation between the Social Security Trust Fund and the U.S. Treasury. The Social Security Trust Fund may have $2.7 trillion of assets, but the only way to get paid is to receive money from the U.S. Treasury, which is already overspending by billions each year. Furthermore, it's effectively impossible to segregate Social Security from the rest of the federal government.

The interrelation of debt between Social Security and the U.S. Treasury is why people can legitimately argue the Social Security Trust Fund doesn't exist, and in some aspects they are correct. It may seem contradictory for both arguments to be correct, but depending upon how you view the Social Security Trust Fund, you can argue its existence or its fabrication.

## The Lockbox

Politicians have adeptly referred to the Social Security Trust Fund as a "lockbox." A lockbox conjures up an image of something which is protected, so when politicians refer to the $2.7 trillion lockbox, you might imagine a huge vault somewhere with large piles of cash, gold, or something tangible contained within it. If only this were true. There is no need for a vault or anything like it, because the $2.7 trillion of assets held Social Security Trust Fund is nothing more than an accounting entry on the books of the federal government.

Another connotation of a lockbox is that it can't be accessed. By employing this type of analogy, our political leaders are trying to assure the American public that the money is set aside for Social Security and can't be used for any other purpose.

The painful irony of the matter is that while politicians have offered guarantees the lockbox is safe and the money can't be used for anything other than paying Social Security benefits, they have had their hands in the cookie jar for decades. All the excess cash received by Social Security has been replaced with IOUs and spent on everything but Social Security (e.g., defense, education, transportation, etc.). For accounting purposes, Social Security monies have not been misappropriated, but for practical purposes, the real dollars collected by Social Security have been spent elsewhere.

At this point in history, it's not worth arguing over the existence of the Social Security Trust Fund or the security of the lockbox. Instead, the focus should be on educating the American public to understand the nature of the Social Security Trust Fund, and more importantly, to address the Treasury's ability to repay money to the Trust Fund.

## The Crossover Date

The crossover date is not an official government term, but it can be defined as the point in time when Social Security expenditures will perpetually exceed revenues. When the crossover date is reached, the

Social Security Trust Fund will continuously redeem its IOUs from the U.S. Treasury to pay the required benefits.

Depending upon how you count revenues, the crossover date may already have happened. As stated in the 2015Trustees' Report, benefit payments exceeded tax revenues by $73billion in 2014 and are estimated to exceed taxes by $68 billion in 2016. Furthermore, there is no time in the future when Social Security taxes are projected to be greater than the benefits being paid, unless tax or benefit changes are enacted.

For the next few years, the Trust Fund will have a small surplus of revenues in excess of benefits paid as a result of interest received on the IOUs from the U.S. Treasury. Even with the inclusion of interest income, the Trustees estimate the crossover date will occur in 2021. Whether it's 2012 (which has already passed) or 2021 (which will soon be upon us), eventually there will come a time when Social Security expenses will forever exceed revenues.

If taken at face value, the crossover date is of little concern in the near term. Social Security will simply redeem some of the loans from the U.S. Treasury to pay the required benefits. However, a long-term challenge arises when the Social Security Trust Fund is fully depleted, which is estimated to be in 2035 according to the 2015 Trustees' Report. When this happens, Social Security won't have enough money to pay current benefits, nor will it have any IOUs from the Treasury to redeem.

For the next couple of decades, Social Security's redemption of its IOUs is not problematic—as long as the U.S. Treasury is able to repay the loans. Although it's unlikely the U.S. government will default on its debt, repayment of the IOUs to Social Security will only increase the current budget deficit and mounting debt.

The federal government has been overspending for decades. For the past 30 years, this overspending has been funded in part by the excess taxes collected from Social Security. When Social Security stops lending its excess cash to the Treasury to fund other government operations and requires repayment of previous loans, the annual deficit and the total debt could rise sharply.

Initially, the total debt may not change, but the lenders will. It's effectively a form of refinancing: the Social Security IOUs must be replaced by other public investors. The Treasury will need to find individuals, institutions, and other nations to lend us an additional $2.7 trillion over a decade to provide the necessary cash to pay Social Security benefits. The amount of additional outside borrowing will be significant. By 2025, the Treasury will need to borrow an extra $228billion each year to meet its obligation to Social Security.

In theory, the deficit won't be impacted until the Social Security Trust Fund is exhausted. While this may be true, the absence of excess Social Security dollars will result in a need for additional outside borrowers, who might demand a higher rate of interest. Beyond any ancillary effects, the annual budget will be directly impacted once the Social Security Trust Fund is exhausted. The 2015 Trustees' Report estimates the benefits paid in 2030 will exceed revenues by $398 billion. Without any Trust Fund to draw from, the general operations of the government would have to fund this obligation. The alternative is to reduce benefits.

The U.S. government may be able to continue spending and borrowing at its current pace without interruption. However, it's unreasonable to assume this can continue forever. Social Security is not supposed to be affected by other government operations, but things may change once the crossover date occurs. Without legislative action, the Treasury will need to borrow money to pay the promised benefits. Should Treasury securities become less desirable, or should it become harder for the federal government to borrow money, it will be more difficult for the U.S. government to pay Social Security benefits and meet all its other obligations.

## Disability Fund Insolvency

Social Security segregates the funds to pay disability from Medicare and retirement funds. Subject to the concerns explained above, the retirement portion of Social Security is not facing an immediate crisis, but the Disability Trust Fund is.

Below is a chart of the Disability Trust Fund receipts, disbursements and asset reserves for the past 15 years.

### Disability Insurance Trust Fund
### 1999-2014
(in millions)

| Calendar Year | Total Receipts | Total Expenditures | Asset Reserves Increase (Decrease) During Year | Asset Reserves at End of Year |
|---|---|---|---|---|
| 1999 | 69,541 | 53,035 | 16,507 | 97,321 |
| 2000 | 77,920 | 56,782 | 21,138 | 118,459 |
| 2001 | 83,903 | 61,369 | 22,534 | 140,993 |
| 2002 | 87,379 | 67,905 | 19,475 | 160,468 |
| 2003 | 88,074 | 73,108 | 14,966 | 175,434 |
| 2004 | 91,380 | 80,597 | 10,783 | 186,217 |
| 2005 | 97,423 | 88,018 | 9,405 | 195,623 |
| 2006 | 102,641 | 94,456 | 8,185 | 203,808 |
| 2007 | 109,854 | 98,778 | 11,076 | 214,884 |
| 2008 | 109,840 | 108,951 | 889 | 215,773 |
| 2009 | 109,283 | 121,506 | (12,223) | 203,550 |
| 2010 | 104,017 | 127,660 | (23,643) | 179,907 |
| 2011 | 106,276 | 132,332 | (26,056) | 153,850 |
| 2012 | 109,115 | 140,299 | (31,184) | 122,666 |
| 2013 | 111,228 | 143,450 | (32,221) | 90,445 |
| 2014 | 114,858 | 145,060 | (30,201) | 60,244 |

Source: http:\\socialsecurity.gov

For several years, the Social Security Trustees have warned that the Disability Fund will be exhausted by the end of 2016. For the past few years, disability payments have exceeded receipts by more than $30 billion each year. With $60 billion of reserves at the end of 2014, it's easy to understand that the Disability Fund has a serious problem.

This is not the first time the Disability Trust Fund has encountered a solvency problem. The Fund was reduced to less than $9 billion in reserves at the end of 1993. However, the excess annual expenditures were $3.3 billion, not $30 billion, which made the correction easier. At the time, Congress adjusted the amount of the disability portion of taxes collected to 1.8% for years after 2000, up from 1.2% in 1993. This is the portion of the total 12.4% of Social Security (OASDI) taxes paid by the employer and employee, or a self-employed person.

The Bipartisan Budget Act of 2015 enacted on November 2, 2015 included several provisions to avoid insolvency of the Disability Fund. Although a number of changes were made to reduce fraudulent claims and confirm benefit eligibility, these changes were not sufficient to erase a $30 billion annual shortfall. To ensure continued solvency, Congress redirected an additional 0.57% of the 12.4% OASDI taxes collected to the Disability Fund for 2016-2018. These changes are intended to make the Disability Fund solvent through 2022.

Although the reallocation of taxes was an easy short-term fix, it will have longer-term implications for Social Security overall. If approximately $30 billion of Social Security taxes are diverted from OASI for the three years, there will be nearly $100 billion less to pay retirement benefits. Such action will accelerate the crossover date and the official insolvency of Social Security before 2035.

## The Bigger Problem

The real risk with the imminent Disability Trust Fund insolvency is not the looming insolvency, the inability to pay disability benefits, or the potential long-term ramifications to OASI from a reallocation of tax revenues. The real problem is the inability and/or unwillingness of Congress and the President to enact a solution in the absence of an immediate crisis.

For years, the Social Security Trustees have been warning of the coming insolvency in their annual report. Despite their warnings and the clear financial pattern, Congress did nothing to correct the problem, nor did they address the long-term solvency issues. They essentially kicked the can down the road for a future President and Congress.

This propensity to avoid proactive solutions doesn't bode well for the entire Social Security system. As challenging as it might be to solve the Disability Trust Fund issue, the dollars pale in comparison to the OASI portion, which will be paying more than $1 trillion in benefits each year by 2020. The sheer magnitude of the dollars involved will make it more difficult to find a palatable economic and political solution. The longer we wait, the more dire the situation and the harder to find a solution.

Unfortunately, Washington's failure to correct the Disability Trust Fund insolvency beyond the next three years, is a precursor to the way our leaders will likely handle the eventual insolvency of the Social Security system.

Summary

Of the current U.S. population of 309 million people, 59 million receive some form of Social Security benefits (19% of the population).

Anything affecting nearly 20% of the population has a significant effect on the culture, government and economy. Not surprisingly, most of those who are currently receiving benefits, or are counting on them in the future, will act to retain their payments.

It's not a question of whether Social Security will exist; it will. The question is what Social Security will be like in the future. Demographic and economic factors of the United States raise significant doubts about the long-term viability of Social Security programs in their current form. Absent any changes, the disability fund will be zeroed out within the next few years and the old-age and survivor fund (i.e., retirement) will be depleted by 2035, assuming the U.S. Treasury can fully repay the $2.7 trillion it borrowed from Social Security. Under any reasonable scenario, disability and retirement benefits will be curtailed in the future unless our political leaders take action.

For some people, their Social Security checks are additional monies they save or spend to support a certain lifestyle. However, for the millions of people who depend on their Social Security checks to survive, any reduction in benefits will create a severe financial hardship.

Social Security involves issues similar to the deficit and debt. The current path is simply unsustainable. It's incumbent upon our political leaders to address the issue and enact changes to make sure Social Security remains in place for the millions of people depending on it to survive. Change will be hard and unpopular, at least to some, but it's necessary. Without it, Social Security as we know it will not exist.

Previous Presidents and Congressional leaders have demonstrated a willingness to cooperate and develop solutions to extend the solvency of Social Security when faced with a crisis. Over the years, they have also undertaken several legislative initiatives to tackle the deficit and debt, but not all these efforts have achieved their intended results.

# CHAPTER 5
# FAILED ATTEMPTS

~~~~~~

Washington, We Have a Problem

The challenges and pitfalls of continuous overspending and a rising national debt have not gone entirely unnoticed in Washington. For decades, Presidents and members of Congress have talked about balancing the budget. They have even gotten beyond political rhetoric and enacted legislation designed to reduce the red ink and eventually balance the budget.

Each attempt was lauded as a solution to get our fiscal house in order. Unfortunately, their good intentions were disconnected from economic realities. Their ultimate fiscal and political decisions overrode whatever desire had existed for fiscal sanity, and each piece of legislation became another failed attempt at buoying the sinking ship.

Although there have been numerous attempts to balance the budget and control federal spending, five major pieces of legislation were enacted over the past four decades in an attempt to significantly alter U.S. fiscal policies.

1)      *Congressional Budget and Impoundment Control Act of 1974.* The Congressional Budget and Impoundment Control Act of

1974 (1974 BCA) created the most sweeping and long-lasting changes to the federal budget process that had been in place since 1921. The following are some of the changes brought about by the 1974 BCA:

- The fiscal year of the U.S. government was changed from July 1 to October 1.

- The House and Senate Budget Committees were created.

- The Congressional Budget Office (CBO) was created to provide Congress with information necessary to formulate a federal budget.

For decades, tensions had existed between the President and Congress over budget and spending priorities. Not surprisingly, the conflict escalated during the late 1960s and early 1970s during the height of the Vietnam War and the era of President Richard Nixon.

One of the greatest sources of discord was President Nixon's decision to impound funds appropriated by Congress. Since the Executive Branch is charged with executing the laws passed by Congress, the President simply directed his staff not to spend certain funds authorized by Congress. He couldn't misappropriate or re-direct the funds, but he could choose not to spend them. The practice of withholding funds is called impoundment.

Presidential impoundment of funds began early in the history of the nation, during the presidency of Thomas Jefferson in 1803. Fearing war would erupt with France, Congress appropriated $50,000 for the construction of 15 gunboats. Jefferson refused to acquire the vessels for two reasons: 1) he thought the existing designs were too expensive and ineffective, and 2) he had dispatched James Madison to France to negotiate a resolution with Napoleon. Jefferson's and Madison's efforts were successful in averting war and ultimately resulted in the Louisiana Purchase.[17]

Impoundment wasn't used again until 1876, by Ulysses S. Grant, as he effectively tried to use impoundment as a line item veto. Franklin D. Roosevelt regularly used impoundment during World War II, and it was used by every subsequent President from Truman through Nixon. Although used sporadically, Nixon greatly expanded the impoundment of funds in an attempt to eliminate or dramatically reduce certain agencies or programs. He directed his staff to withhold as much as 20% of funds appropriated by Congress for certain programs.

Congress re-exerted its power of the purse by restricting presidential power to impound funds. As a result of the 1974 BCA, the President was required to notify Congress if he wanted to delay the expenditure of funds, and either chamber could disapprove at any time. In order to eliminate funding, the House and Senate had to affirmatively approve the rescission. The intent of the 1974 BCA was to force the President to spend the monies appropriated by Congress.[18]

The 1974 BCA was also the first modern attempt by Congress to reduce federal spending by giving Congress more time to enact a budget and alter the process. According to the Budget and Accounting Act of 1921, the President must deliver his proposed budget to Congress by the first Monday in February. Congress changed the fiscal year from July 1 to October 1 to give them more time to deliberate and pass the necessary appropriation bills. The 1974 BCA called for the Budget Committees to pass a first resolution by May 15 and the second by September 15, before the fiscal year began on October 1.[19] The extra three months were supposed to give Congress sufficient time to pass timely appropriation bills and eliminate the use of continuing resolutions.

Additionally, the 1974 BCA changed the structure of the appropriation bills passed by Congress. Prior to 1974, Congress voted on separate bills for revenues and appropriations. Under the 1974 BCA, all revenues, appropriations and authorizations would be considered one bill. The architects of the 1974 BCA assumed lawmakers would vote differently if they considered the budget as a whole, rather than disconnecting revenue from spending.

Except for halting Presidential impoundment and the formation of the Budget Committees and the CBO, the long-term results of the 1974 BCA were exactly the opposite of what was originally intended. The consolidation of the various budget measures into one bill has allowed the President to exert more control over the process. Now he only has to deal with one big piece of legislation rather than negotiating and passing many small ones. Congress also benefited from consolidating the budget process; it's harder to strip funding for pork barrel projects from large must-pass legislative measures.

Changing the fiscal year to October 1 and shifting the resolution time frames have had little impact on the timing for passing budgets and appropriation bills. The reliance upon continuing resolutions to fund the government has increased over the past few years as the President and Congress have been unable to reach an agreement on spending and revenue by October 1, if at all.

After passing a budget in April 2009, the Senate didn't pass a budget for nearly four years. During this time, the Senate did not even bring a budget resolution to the floor for a vote. It's unlikely the authors of the 1974 BCA could have even imagined Congress failing to pass a budget measure for nearly four years.

At the time of passing the 1974 BCA, some members of Congress were also concerned about ongoing budget deficits and inadequate controls over entitlement programs. The 1974 BCA was intended to help Congress re-exert its authority over federal spending, but also to improve the controls over spending.

The concerns of Congress in the early 1970s pale in comparison to what has generally transpired over the past four decades. Total federal spending has far outpaced inflation, and annual budget deficits have exploded, both in nominal and real dollars. Sadly, the problems the 93rd Congress sought to address with the 1974 BCA have grown exponentially over the past four decades.

2)    *Balanced Budget and Emergency Deficit Control Act (1985).* This legislation quickly became known as the Gramm-Rudman-Hollings Act, reflecting the names of the three principal sponsors. Passed in 1985, the overall intent of the law was to reduce the budget deficit to zero by 1991. In order to achieve this goal within such a short time frame, the law established a maximum allowable

annual budget deficit over the following six years. If Congress and the President were unable to adopt a budget meeting a specific target, across-the-board spending cuts in most federal programs would have automatically been triggered (i.e., sequestration). This was intended to provide all parties with an incentive to reach an agreement and avoid dramatic spending cuts in programs they deemed vital.[20]

The legislation relied upon the Comptroller General to certify that the budget met the deficit target. The Comptroller General heads the General Accounting Office and is under the dominion and control of Congress. The selection of the Comptroller General ultimately led to the law being declared unconstitutional by the U.S. Supreme Court in 1986.

The Supreme Court ignored the general intent and workings of the law and focused on the role of the Comptroller General. The separation of powers enumerated in the Constitution gave Congress the power to pass legislation, and the President the power to implement the laws. Since the Comptroller General serves Congress rather than the President, the Court ruled that the Comptroller General's role was part of the implementation of the law. As an agent of Congress, the Court determined their role an unconstitutional violation of the separation of powers.

Congress amended the law in 1987 to transfer the role from the Comptroller General to the OMB, with advisory input by the CBO. They also revised the deficit targets and extended the date for balancing the budget. The automatic spending cuts were applied in

1990, but subsequently repealed in 1991 after an agreement between Congress and President George H.W. Bush.

It appears Senators Gramm, Rudman and Hollings grasped the nature of Washington politics when drafting the legislation. The law provided for a schedule of annual budget deficit targets. Congress has a propensity to frontload revenue and backload spending cuts in legislation, but history has proven that future spending cuts are seldom realized. Without a predetermined schedule of annual targets, Congress might have done little in the first few years after the legislation, with the intention of implementing the spending cuts in future years. Graham-Rudman-Hollings enacted specific budget parameters preventing Congress from deferring current budget cuts.

The senators also recognized the need for some type of verification. Even though the law didn't fully address the consequences if the final deficit was different from the projected deficit, it initially required the Comptroller General to certify that the budget met specific targets. This was intended to keep Congress and the President honest, reflecting an implicit acknowledgment that Washington politicians are not always the most honest and trustworthy people.

An argument can be made that Gramm-Rudman-Hollings was not a complete failure. Aside from the necessary changes following the Supreme Court decision in 1986, Congress revised the law to reduce the necessary cuts and extend the date for finally achieving a balanced budget. The budget was eventually balanced in 2000, nine years after the original target of 1991. With the economic recession following the bursting of the tech bubble in the late 1990s, the government started racking up deficits in 2001, and has done so every year since. Balancing the budget for one year was clearly not the intent of the law, but it did curtail spending and contributed to the federal government balancing its budget for the first time in decades.

Although it can be prudent to revise plans as facts and circumstances change, this effort highlights the propensity of Congress to defer difficult decisions. The political climate in Washington hasn't improved in the past 30 years. In 1985, Gramm-Rudman-Hollings set a target of balancing the budget in six years; today, even the most ardent fiscal conservatives talk of balancing the budget in no fewer than ten years.

3)      *Budget Enforcement Act of 1990.* Faced with a budget deficit that would not meet the target established by the Gramm-Rudman-Hollings Act, Congress and President George H.W. Bush reached an agreement: The Budget Enforcement Act of 1990 (BEA 1990). BEA 1990 brought several changes to the budget process:

1.  It revised the budget deficit targets of Gramm-Rudman Hollings Act for Fiscal 1991 through 1995.
2.  It created caps on annually appropriated spending.
3.  It established an order for sequestration under the Gramm-Rudman-Hollings Act.
4.  It mandated a "pay-as-you-go" (PAYGO) process for entitlements and taxes.[21]

One of the primary reasons for passing BEA 1990 was the inability of Congress and President Bush to craft a budget that would meet the Gramm-Rudman-Hollings Act deficit targets. As such, it's no surprise that BEA 1990 weakened the controls which could have led to a balanced budget by the early 1990s.

BEA 1990 was amended several times and finally expired in 2002. Along with the Gramm-Rudman-Hollings Act, BEA 1990 was a contributing factor to the achievement of a balanced budget in 2000. However, the long-term effect was little more than a blip on the budget deficit horizon. A one-year balanced budget was not what the proponents had in mind when the legislation was passed.

BEA 1990 was a clear example of how our national leaders can alter legislation at their will to avoid certain consequences. While the principle of change and flexibility is not necessarily bad, perpetually avoiding difficult choices is. The ability to change laws and the inability to make unpopular decisions are precisely the reasons the U.S. has only achieved a balanced budget once in the past 40 years.

The PAYGO concept is probably the most lasting impact of BEA 1990. The PAYGO principles were codified into law with the Statutory Pay-As-You-Go Act of 2010.

4)      *The Line Item Veto Act of 1996.* Since shortly after the founding of the nation, presidents have wanted a line item veto. It's hard to know if the Founding Fathers expected or anticipated the politicking involved in spending taxpayers' money. Had they understood the political machinations of the process, they may have

included a line item veto in the Constitution. Alternatively, they may have intentionally excluded a line item veto to prevent one person from having too much power over government taxation and spending.

Although the President submits a proposed budget, Congress has the responsibility and authority for drafting the budget and appropriation bills. The President can offer input and try to influence the outcome, but his role in the process is limited. Once Congress passes the bill, the President must either sign or veto the bill. At that point, he either accepts or rejects every dollar being spent. The only way to eliminate one spending item is to reject the entire bill. Faced with such a choice, the President usually signs it into law.

Most presidents would cherish the ability to veto selected expenditures without having to reject everything else. With this power, the President could negotiate over the necessity and propriety of the struck items rather than having to contend with all items at once.

The ability to veto selected items would clearly increase the President's power over federal spending and diminish Congressional power; thus, it's understandable why Congress is reticent to grant the President a line item veto, which might reduce their power.

Two types of items that presidents might want to veto and negotiate are pork barrel spending and earmarks. Pork barrel spending refers to the act of an elected official directing government spending to his or her representative district in order to garner the support of constituents. Earmarks are similar in that they bypass the appropriations process and Executive Branch management by directing funds to be spent for a specific purpose or group. Earmarks can also be included in legislative bills or committee reports, which make them much less transparent.

Since Congress needs a certain number of votes to pass legislation, pork barrel spending and earmarks are frequently included as a manner of gaining the necessary votes. As the effectiveness and success of politicians has increasingly been measured by their ability to "bring home the bacon," the use of earmarks and pork barrel spending has increased dramatically.

The "Bridge to Nowhere" is a prime example of earmarks. Three separate earmarks allocated $320 million to build a bridge between Ketchikan, Alaska (population 9,000) and the Island of Gravina (population 50). People could access the island via ferry, but they wanted a bridge to avoid the $6 toll and a 15-30 minute wait to cross. Amid a national embarrassment over this project, Congress reallocated 70% of the funds to help with reconstruction after Hurricane Katrina struck the Gulf Coast.[22]

Support for the National Cowboy Poetry Gathering in Elko, Nevada is another expenditure many criticize as wasteful government spending. Reasonable people can debate the value of spending money to support the arts, and the grant from the National Endowment for the Arts doesn't fully fund the event. The grant became a political issue after Senator Harry Reid, the Majority Leader at the time, claimed "tens of thousands of people" attended the event each year, even though the sponsoring organization estimates annual attendance at 6,000-8,000.[23]

Despite the value to the constituents benefitting from these expenditures, the President might think they are not the best use of taxpayer funds. With a line item veto, he could strike these specific appropriations and accept the rest of the funds approved by Congress. Without it, he must either veto the entire bill or allow the spending to remain. Congress knows the President is reticent to veto billions of dollars in federal spending over small matters—they count on it.

The lack of a line item veto is probably what led presidents to impound funds. The funds had been approved, but the President refused to spend the money allocated. Presidents used the power of impoundment sparingly for the first 200 years of the Republic, which limited its impact. As explained earlier, once President Nixon began using impoundment to impact major budget appropriations, Congress passed the 1974 BCA to neutralize the presidential power of impoundment.

Legislation for a line item veto was first introduced to Congress in 1876. Congress finally passed a line-time veto bill 120 years later, when President Bill Clinton signed the Line Item Veto Act of 1996. Interestingly, the legislation made it through Congress when Republicans controlled the House and Senate, and President Clinton was a Democrat, proving that on occasion, Washington can bridge the partisan divide to address a controversial matter.

The following is a brief summary of the mechanics of the Line Item Veto Act:

1. Congress passes an appropriations bill.
2. The President strikes certain provisions and signs the modified legislation.
3. Congress has 30 days to vote to reinstate the appropriation by passing another bill by a simple majority vote.
4. The President can veto the bill restoring the expenditure.
5. Congress can override the President's veto by a two-thirds majority vote of both houses.[24]

Under the 1974 BCA, the President had to seek Congressional approval to withhold any appropriated funds. The Line Item Veto Act shifted the burden of action from the President to Congress. Once the President struck an expenditure via a line item veto, the money would not be spent unless Congress voted to reinstate it.

Although Congress approved the legislation, support was not unanimous. Immediately after passage, several Democratic Senators and Representatives filed suit against the law. In 1998, the U.S. Supreme Court declared the law to be unconstitutional. The Court found the President's ability to strike certain portions of an appropriations bill violated the legislative process created by the U.S. Constitution.

Congress should be commended for passing the Line Item Veto Act 120 years after the measure was first introduced. However, Senators and Representatives were also at the forefront of overturning the measure. While these duly-elected members of Congress had legitimate Constitutional concerns about the legislation, they also enjoyed the advantages of the appropriations process and didn't want to see their influenced diminished. Congressional influence is power in Washington, and nothing demonstrates power like the ability to direct federal spending.

Despite their political rhetoric denouncing wasteful government spending, Congress likes the ability to insert earmarks and add pork barrel spending into legislation. It makes their constituents happy, which increases their likelihood of being re-elected. If Congress truly opposed to the practice, they would end it. They don't need a line item veto to accomplish it. Instead, Congressional leaders could modify the budget and appropriations process to eliminate or greatly reduce targeted or expenditures of questionable value. Since virtually every Senator and Representative engages in the practice to some extent, there is little incentive to change it. Why fix a broken system when it works well for incumbent politicians?

5)      *Pay-As-You-Go Act of 2010.* The Pay-As-You-Go Act of 2010 (PAYGO) was not intended to reduce or increase the budget. The goal of PAYGO was budget neutrality. PAYGO requires that bills which reduce existing federal revenues must have equal offsetting cuts to mandatory spending, or provide for an equal amount of new revenues. Similarly, any bills increasing mandatory spending must be offset by cuts in other mandatory expenditures or revenue must be

raised to pay for the additional spending. For PAYGO purposes, bills affecting mandatory spending or taxes are treated the same.

The OMB is given the responsibility of scoring legislation affected by PAYGO. If Congress adjourns session with approved legislation bearing costs that increase the deficit, across-the-board spending cuts (sequestration) must be applied to certain mandatory programs in an amount sufficient to offset the excess costs calculated under PAYGO.

The following programs are exempt from sequestration:

- Social Security
- Most unemployment benefits
- Veterans' benefits
- Interest on the debt
- Federal retirement benefits
- Low-income entitlements such as Medicaid and SNAP (food stamps)

The law also provides Congress with several spending increases that are exempt from PAYGO.

- Social Security and the U.S. Postal Service
- Emergency costs
- Shifting revenues or expenses outside the 10-year budget projection to avoid PAYGO
- CLASS Act costs or savings (certain prefunded long-term care benefits)
- Current scorekeeping adjustments, unless changed by future legislation[25]

Since passing PAYGO, Congress and the President have managed the federal government without increasing the deficit—or at least that is what they will tell you. This is true, according to their rules and "fuzzy math."

Since enacting the law, Congress has continually invoked the emergency clause to increase spending. Emergency spending doesn't require offsetting revenues, and the additional expenditures are not counted as increasing the deficit. In 2010, Congress increased unemployment benefits, health care subsidies, and extended a number of programs that had expired. Within the first year of PAYGO, Congress exempted approximately $2-3 trillion of spending over the following ten years simply by dubbing it emergency spending.

PAYGO embraces a simply financial principle: don't spend money you don't have. It's a principle millions of Americans follow, but it continually eludes Congress. With a simple declaration that something is an "emergency," Congress avoids the difficult choice of cutting existing spending or raising additional revenue. As an added bonus, they can claim they haven't voted to increase the deficit, despite the reality of spending more money. Such is the way of Washington.

## Summary

The various instances of budget and spending control legislation enacted over the past 40 years were designed to reduce spending and limit the total debt incurred. Though well intended, these measures became a series of failed attempts to rein in federal spending. In spite of these efforts, the national debt exceeds $18 trillion and annual budget deficits totaling $500 billion to more than $1 trillion have become normal.

Our national leaders can parrot a myriad of reasons the money needed to be spent. There have been numerous unexpected and unplanned events and disasters drawing upon the federal coffers, and some truly have been emergencies. Although the severity and magnitude may vary, there is nothing new about economic cycles of growth and recession, or the occurrence of hurricanes, tornados, earthquakes and other natural disasters.

Although situations and rationalizations change, one thing remains unchanged: overspending by the U.S. government. Congress' previous attempts to control spending and balance the budget demonstrate an awareness of the problem, but more is required. Congress and the President must stop justifying their decisions to circumvent the controls they put in place, balance the budget, and eventually start to repay the debt.

# CHAPTER 6
# AFFORDABLE CARE ACT

<u>Overview</u>

Much like the Social Security chapter, it may seem inappropriate to include The Patient Protection and Affordable Care Act, commonly referred to as the Affordable Care Act (ACA) or Obamacare in a book dedicated to the deficit and the debt. Since there are several components of the ACA paid by the U.S. government, there are current and future budget implications associated with the ACA.

According to many politicians and the initial CBO scoring of the legislation, the ACA does not cost the federal government money during the first decade. As previously stated, politicians are excellent illusionists and economic realities are often quite different from what is being stated, which raises questions about the budget neutrality of the ACA.

The ACA was, is, and will be a highly controversial, partisan and emotional issue for the nation. Many complex issues and topics are being debated, most of which are outside the purview of this book, but some are not. Tax, spending, and budgetary provisions are part of the ACA. Any legislation that impacts all U.S. citizens and one-sixth of the U.S. economy has major fiscal implications for the nation. These are the topics addressed in this chapter.

None of the ACA provisions were effective before January 1, 2013, so it is difficult to draw conclusions on the fiscal effects of the law. Therefore, the primary purpose of this section is highlighting the provisions of the law that could cost the federal government much more than originally estimated.

## History and Background

The Patient Protection and Affordable Care Act, more commonly referred to as the Affordable Care Act (ACA) or Obamacare, was signed by President Obama on March 23, 2010. The legislation enacted the most significant changes to the American healthcare system since the founding of the Republic. The text of the bill was more than 1,000 pages long and the subsequent regulations are equally voluminous, with some still being drafted.

A primary goal of the legislation is increasing the number of people covered by insurance, thus reducing the number of uninsured. The following provisions are intended to accomplish this objective:

- Provide incentives for states to expand the number of people covered by Medicaid,
- Require certain employers to provide affordable coverage to their employees, or pay fines,
- Require individuals to have health insurance, or pay a tax (penalty),
- Provide subsidies and tax credits to help employers and individuals afford the premiums,

- Prohibit insurers from charging premiums based upon pre-existing conditions or sex, and
- Establish health care exchanges to assistant individuals in purchasing health care coverage from different insurers.

The legislation also required insurance companies to meet certain minimum coverage standards for all policies, including:

- Eliminating any lifetime cap on the amount of medical benefits provided,
- Allowing children to remain on their parents' policies until age 26,
- Prohibiting insurance companies from voluntarily terminating coverage, and
- Requiring coverage for certain preventative procedures and prescriptions.

At the time of passage, the CBO scored the ACA as being budget neutral, which will be discussed later in this chapter. Some of the legislated revenue mechanisms included to contribute to neutrality are:

- Penalties assessed to individuals who do not have adequate insurance coverage,
- Taxes levied against employers who fail to cover their employees,
- A tax on the sale of medical equipment and devices,
- Limitations placed on individual taxpayers' deduction of qualified medical expenses,

- Limits placed on the deduction for compensation paid to executives of insurance companies, and

- Imposition of a tax upon insurance policies with overly generous insurance coverage (AKA "Cadillac policies").

The legislation was highly controversial before its passage, and this has not changed in the past five years. The debate will likely continue for the foreseeable future. Many lawsuits have also been filed challenging various aspects of the law, and more litigation can be expected.

On June 28, 2012, The U.S. Supreme Court upheld the fundamental provisions of the ACA in *National Federation of Independent Business* v. *Sebelius*. A major constitutional question was presented to the Court: Could the U.S. government penalize its citizens for failing to engage in a specific commercial activity (i.e., the purchase of health insurance)? In finding the individual mandate constitutional, the Court determined the shared responsibility payment was effectively not a penalty but a tax, which was well within Congress' taxing power. However, unlike any other federal tax, the government doesn't have the power to enforce payment, other than garnishing future tax refunds. In all other tax levies, the IRS can enforce payment through fines, penalties, collection procedures, and even criminal prosecution.

The other major aspect of the case involved Medicaid funding. Part of the plan for extending insurance coverage to all U.S. citizens included a significant expansion in Medicaid (insurance for low-income people). Although the short-term costs were to be fully paid by the federal government, many state leaders were concerned about the potential long-term costs and impact on state budgets. The original legislation attempted to force states to expand Medicaid coverage by threatening to withhold current Medicaid funding for any state refusing the expansion. The Supreme Court found this to be an unconstitutional infringement on the sovereign rights of states.

There have been, and likely will be, varied attempts to repeal or replace the law, but it's doubtful any meaningful changes will happen in the near future. Many commentators attribute the ACA as the signature achievement of President Obama's first term and doubt he will consent to major alterations to the law. For example, Congress passed the Restoring Americans' Healthcare Freedom Reconciliation Act of 2015, which would have repealed critical elements of the ACA and rendered it ineffective. President Obama vetoed the bill two days after it passed on January 6, 2016. Although certain revisions may be made, no substantial changes are expected until after President Obama leaves office, if ever.

Budget Neutrality

As previously discussed in the deficit chapter, CBO scoring determines whether legislation increases or decreases the cumulative deficit over the following ten years. CBO scoring can be a rather benign process relegated to the halls of Congress, but with the ACA it was thrust into the forefront of the debate. As political battles over the

ACA continue, CBO scoring will continue to be used by opponents and proponents to bolster their arguments.

The initial ACA legislation was introduced in 2009, during the depths of the Great Recession. The budget deficit had exploded to more than $1 trillion annually, and the country had already amassed more than $12 trillion in debt. Times were tough and there was no certainty of when the economy would improve, and if so, by how much.

In many respects, the ACA was the largest expansion of a government entitlement program since the passage of Medicare in 1965. Understandably, there was significant concern that implementing the ACA would cost the federal government billions, or even trillions, of additional dollars it didn't have. Consequently, the CBO score became a significant topic of debate and weighed into the consideration of whether the ACA would pass through Congress.

By itself, the CBO score wasn't likely to convince Congress to vote in favor of or against the ACA. A budget neutral or reduction score wouldn't ensure passage, but a CBO determination that the ACA added to the deficit and debt would be another hurdle to clear. Proponents of the legislation were very happy when the CBO reported the ACA was projected to reduce federal spending by more than $100 billion over the following ten years. The CBO score bolstered the argument that the ACA would reduce the future growth rate for health care costs.

Like many aspects of the ACA, the CBO score was not without controversy. Opponents were suspicious of the CBO conclusion that adding millions of people to Medicaid was going to save the government money. While the CBO is a nonpartisan agency of Congress, it only scores legislation according to the rules determined by Congress, as previously explained.

## Stealing from Medicare

The ACA is supposed to extend the solvency of Medicare by nearly a decade. The law contained two Medicare tax increases: (1) taxpayers with earned income in excess of $200,000 ($250,000 for married taxpayers) would be subject to an additional 0.9% tax on their earnings, and (2) taxpayers with adjusted gross income (AGI) in excess of $250,000 would also be subject to a 3.8% tax on their investment earnings (e.g., interest, dividends and capital gains). These revenues clearly contribute to Medicare's solvency by adding more tax revenues to the program.

The idea of raising Medicare taxes to support the program seems rather straightforward, but Washington politicking and accounting alter a simple concept. The additional taxes raised by Medicare won't remain within the Social Security and Medicare Trust fund for long. Once again, the Treasury will "loan" the additional funds to the general operating funds of the government to help pay for the costs of the ACA.[26] The Treasury will issue more intragovernmental debt for the borrowed money. These additional loans will add to the existing $2.7 trillion already owed to the Social Security Trust Fund.

113

With millions of Baby Boomers attaining Medicare eligibility each year, the demand for repayment of these loans will come quickly. Since the money will have already been spent, the Treasury will be forced to borrow more money to repay the money borrowed from Medicare. It's the same issue involving the Social Security lockbox, as explained in the chapter on Social Security.

Lending the additional Medicare taxes from the Social Security Trust Fund has resulted in political accusations of $500 billion being stolen from Medicare to fund the ACA. These allegations are used for political theater, and for swaying voters for a particular candidate, but they are not legally accurate. It's simply the same mechanism that has allowed the Social Security Trust Fund to accumulate $2.7 trillion of intragovernmental debt. There is nothing illegal about this practice, but it raises questions about government spending and the ability to repay the funds in the future.

Once again, Congress is using excess current revenues to fund immediate spending with the promise to repay the funds in the future. It's not a realistic expectation that the cost of the ACA or Medicare will decrease in the future. Consequently, a day of reckoning will eventually arise when additional Medicare taxes are needed to pay Medicare expenses, and the ACA costs have continued to increase. When this happens, Congress will be pressed either to find other sources of revenue, or to issue more debt to pay the ACA costs.

## Double-Counting Medicare Savings

In addition to the accusation of robbing from Medicare, some critics have accused the CBO of double-counting the Medicare savings in making their determination that the ACA will reduce the deficit over the next decade. There is some validity to the argument, but it is complex to unravel. Below is a brief and simplistic synopsis.

- The additional taxes are specifically allocated to Medicare, which extends the solvency of Medicare, but

- In the immediate future, the additional taxes will be loaned from the Social Security Trust Fund to the general Treasury funds to pay for the ACA.

- The CBO assumes the funds will be repaid to the Social Security Trust fund at some future date, likely beyond the ten-year time horizon.

- According to the government accounting and the scoring principles used by the CBO, the additional Medicare taxes are included in the ACA revenues to calculate deficit neutrality.

Since the same dollars are being counted as extending Medicare, while simultaneously funding the ACA, the double-counting charge has some legitimacy. However, according to CBO scoring guidelines and government accounting practices, the official report doesn't treat the funds as double-counted.

Recall the role of the CBO described in Chapter 2. The CBO is the scorekeeper for Congress, who makes the rules. The principle against counting the same income twice may be a basic financial and budgeting principle, but it's possible using the arcane accounting and budgetary process of the U.S. government. By understanding its own rules, Congress was able to write the ACA legislation in such a way that led the CBO to the desired conclusion.

Such practices are typical of the way Washington works, and these techniques were prevalent in drafting the ACA. Dr. Jonathan Gruber, an MIT economist who advocated for and consulted on the drafting of the ACA, publicly admitted in October 2013 that the legislation was drafted in a "tortured manner" to avoid the individual mandate being classified as a tax while the bill was being debated. However, while defending the ACA before the U.S. Supreme Court, the U.S. Solicitor General argued that the mandate was a tax. The Court agreed with the Solicitor General's argument in its opinion upholding the law. While not specifically addressing the double-counting of Medicare savings, this is indicative of how Washington leaders manipulate legislation and defy logic to arrive at a specific result.

## Current CBO Scoring

Nearly four years after the ACA's passage, the CBO dropped its claim that the ACA will reduce federal spending over the next decade. They have yet to declare that the ACA will increase the deficit. In an April 2014 report, they indicated that the numerous changes and delays to the law have essentially made it impossible to calculate the long-term budgetary impact of the ACA.

The CBO's inability to score the cost of the ACA will add to the political drama surrounding the ACA, but there is a greater unidentified cost. Even though the scoring process is often manipulated to arrive at a predetermined conclusion, the CBO is supposed to provide financial information to Congress in order for senators and representatives to make well-informed decisions. The CBO's inability to score the ACA leaves a vacuum of credible independent information, which will be filled with more partisan political rhetoric.

Their lack of a definitive conclusion of the budgetary costs is understandable, but it also highlights the future challenges and fiscal risk of the ACA. If Congress passed a bill that's too complex for Washington policy wonks to adequately understand, how do they expect the average American citizen to understand and comply with it? Furthermore, the real long-term cost could be much different than what was originally projected; most of the revenue raising provisions are already in effect, but many of the costs have yet to be incurred.

It's far too early to know how accurate the CBO scoring models were. Future financial results will provide those answers. However, it's a warning sign and a concern that four years after passage, the CBO can no longer score the cost of the legislation.

Bending the Cost Curve

The ACA is supposed to help reduce the long-term cost of providing health care to everyone in the U.S. For the last 20 years, health care costs have increased at nearly twice the cost of all other goods and services bought in the U.S. Reducing the long-term rate of inflation is commonly referenced as "bending the cost curve."

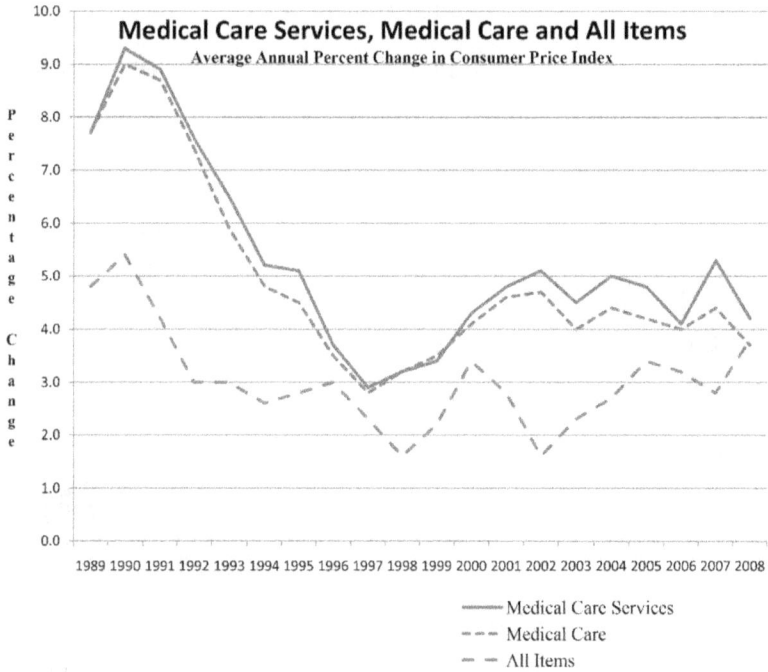

From 1989 through 2008, the average annual inflation rate of health care services was 5.3%. The average inflation rate for all U.S. goods and services during the same period was 3.0%. [27] While an additional 2.3% per year may not seem like much, the cumulative compounding of this is quite dramatic. If you pay $100 for a medical bill today, it will cost you $134 in ten years if the annual inflation rate is 3.0%. If the annual inflation rate is 5.3%, the cost jumps to $168.

The difference may be negligible for $100, but considering that the U.S. spent more than $3 trillion on health care costs in 2014,[28] the difference in inflation rates can equate to more than $3.8 trillion of additional spending over the next decade. Therefore, bending the cost curve even slightly can result in billions of dollars in future savings.

How does the ACA bend the cost curve? Providing medical insurance coverage to all American citizens is supposed to be the primary generator of cost savings. The argument is as follows:

- Prior to the ACA, uninsured people often couldn't afford routine health care.
- Without a primary care doctor, they frequently visited the Emergency Room for all health care needs, which is typically more expensive than out-of-hospital care.
- Without insurance, many of these patients couldn't afford the medical services provided.
- Medical providers would often be forced to heavily discount or write off substantial portions of the bills incurred by uninsured patients.
- Medical providers would then increase their future rates to compensate for the uncollectible accounts, increasing the costs for those who had insurance.
- Thus, if every person had insurance coverage, there would be no more cost shifting, and the overall cost of medical care would decline for everyone.

Beyond expansion of coverage to all Americans, the long-term cost of coverage would also be reduced through:

- Agreements reached with pharmaceutical companies regarding pricing of medication.

- Paying health care providers for performance, rather than services rendered. This led to accusations of rationing care and "death panels." Beyond the more inflammatory comments, medical care is not an exact science and it can be difficult to determine which procedures are necessary.

- Limitations on future reimbursement rates to medical providers. While good in theory, the practice is much more difficult to implement. As described in Chapter 2, legislation has existed for years to reduce the Medicare and Medicaid reimbursement rate for doctors, yet it has continually been extended for fear too many doctors would no longer agree to treat Medicare patients. The potential risk is magnified when reimbursement rates are decreased for even more patients.

Medical care costs have risen well above the average annual inflation rate for the past two decades. Bending the cost curve for health care is a worthy objective and would benefit all Americans. The ACA may achieve this objective, but it's too early to be certain, and there are some reasonable objections and questions about the underlying assumptions and implementation.

## Waivers and Delays

Given the scope and complexity of the ACA, it really shouldn't be a surprise that the implementation of the law has been less than smooth. The 2013 rollout of the enrollment website for the federal health insurance exchange was a major disaster and embarrassment for the Obama Administration. Despite the billions spent to develop the website, it was cumbersome, unreliable, and at times simply not functional. The inability of people to enroll and purchase health insurance led to multiple delays in the enrollment deadline and implementation of the individual mandate (i.e., the penalty/tax assessed for not obtaining adequate insurance as of January 1, 2014).

The situation was so problematic that the administration effectively eliminated the individual mandate for 2014 by granting a "hardship exemption" if a person "experienced another hardship in obtaining health insurance." Without defining "another hardship," it appears the administration granted a vague exemption for anyone not purchasing insurance.

The employer mandate was also extended twice. The first delay was issued in July 2013, deferring until 2015 the penalties against all employers with more than 50 employees who failed to offer the required coverage. Another delay was granted to employers who employed between 50 and 100 employees until 2016 to meet the coverage requirements.

Between the individual hardship exemption and delays to the employer mandate, the requirements to provide or purchase coverage were effectively been pushed to 2015 and beyond. Further delays could be forthcoming if problems with the federal exchange enrollment website aren't adequately addressed as the future enrollment deadlines approach.

In addition to delaying certain provisions of the ACA, the Department of Health and Human Services (HHS) has issued more than a thousand waivers to employers with health plans that don't meet the requirements of the ACA. Most of the waivers are intended to be temporary. HHS may be less willing to grant waivers once the employer and individual mandates are enforced and the health care exchanges are fully operational. For now, though, employers are able to escape the penalties associated with nonconforming plans through these waivers.

Supporters of the ACA have defended the delays and waivers as routine and necessary events in implementing significant new legislation. Opponents seized on these topics to continue their attacks on the ACA. They also argued that President Obama exceeded his executive authority and rewrote legislation through the delays and waivers. Congressional Republicans have filed suit against the President for delaying the employer mandate, contending there is nothing in the legislation giving the President the unilateral right to delay the mandate and defer the collection of the associated penalties.

There are many legal and political issues involved which are outside the scope of *A Sinking Nation*. However, the waivers and delays have a financial impact on the revenues collected by the U.S. Treasury. In attempting to provide an updated score of the ACA, the CBO found the number of waivers and delays have made it impossible to calculate an accurate score. The fiscal impact of the waivers and delays may be minimal, but they have raised the likelihood that the

ACA won't reduce the deficit by the amount originally predicted by the CBO.

Delays and waivers have effectively eliminated the assessment of penalties, thereby reducing the revenues expected to be generated by the ACA. Although the intent of the law was for all to comply, the CBO projected some level of noncompliance and counted the penalties as additional revenues to the federal government. A delay in the enforcement of penalties reduces the projected revenues collected under the ACA. This concept is similar to the assessment of "sin taxes" (i.e., taxes on alcohol and tobacco). The government assesses a tax on these products because they are deemed harmful to health and society. Even though the taxes are intended to increase the cost of these products and reduce consumption, governmental entities plan for these tax revenues, and state and local governments frequently raise sin taxes to help balance their budgets. While the increased cost may provide an additional deterrent to engaging in the "sinful" activity, the primary objective is additional tax revenues.

## Insurance Companies

The ACA mandates are intended to add millions of Americans to the insurance companies' customer rolls, thus increasing total premiums by billions of dollars. With the required expansion of their customer base, it's easy to understand support for the ACA among insurance company executives. However, the rapid expansion of insured people and coverage requirements also introduces significant financial risk.

Insurance is a combination of pooling and reallocation of resources. Financially, insurance is a bad investment unless tragedy strikes. As a homeowner, it's highly unlikely you will experience a fire or the complete destruction of your home. If you never have a claim, you will have paid thousands of dollars to an insurance company with no return. On the other hand, the premiums could be the bargain of a lifetime if you suffer a tragedy.

Insurance companies make money and stay in business by collecting premiums from a lot of people and paying large sums of money to only a few. Miscalculating the difference can cause huge financial losses for the insurance company, and continuous losses will put the company out of business. As a consumer, you want your premiums to be as cheap as possible, but you also want the insurance company to pay when you have a claim. The last thing you want is for an insurance company to become insolvent when you need to collect from them.

Actuaries crunch the numbers for insurance companies to determine the premiums required for the company to remain profitable. Before implementation of the ACA, insurance companies used demographic and economic statistics, often compiled over decades, to assess future claims and the premiums necessary to pay them. Three provisions were included in the ACA to mitigate the risks to insurance companies from the sudden change in actuarial data:[29]

1) *Risk Adjustment Provision.* Insurance companies historically denied coverage or charged higher premiums based on the

health status or habits of their customers. The ACA eliminates many of these health assessments and requires insurance companies to charge the same premium to everyone. The ACA acknowledged that people with more serious health care needs have a greater incentive to obtain health care coverage, which could end up costing insurance companies a lot of money.

The Risk Adjustment Provision (RAP) was designed to reduce an insurance company's incentive to avoid enrolling people requiring more health services by sharing the risk with its peers. Insurance companies with more low-cost enrollees contribute to a fund which is paid to other insurance companies with more high-cost enrollees. It's essentially a cost-sharing mechanism among insurance companies and is not supposed to have any cost to the federal government.

2)    *Transitional Reinsurance Provision.* Under the ACA, pre-existing conditions and medical history generally have no impact on the premiums charged for a particular enrollee. Therefore, it was anticipated that currently uninsured people with existing or anticipated high medical costs would have a greater incentive to enroll in ACA coverage immediately, while healthy people and those with minimal medical needs might defer enrollment. If these dynamics held true, early enrollment demographics might not be reflective of the overall population and long-term enrollment.

The Transitional Reinsurance Provision (TRP) was designed to prevent insurers from avoiding higher risk individuals, and to stabilize insurance premiums in the early years of the ACA. Similar to the RAP, the funds are collected from all health insurance premiums and are used to compensate insurance providers.

Unlike the RAP, the TRP assessment is charged to all providers of insurance plans, not just insurance companies. Therefore, employers and other entities that sponsor plans or self-insure contribute to the cost. The TRP also has specific financial parameters: it will compensate an insurer of an individual policy 80% of the cost of annual health claims between $45,000 and $250,000. The TRP is expected to collect $10 billion in 2014. The Department of Health and Human Services (HHS) will readjust these reimbursement parameters to make sure payments don't exceed the funds collected. Accordingly, the TRP is supposed to be budget neutral (i.e., it has no effect on the federal budget).

3)     *Temporary Risk Corridor Program.* The Temporary Risk Corridor Program (TRCP) is the risk-sharing mechanism that has garnered the most attention and press. The TRCP is often referred to as a bailout for insurance companies. Since government bailouts have a very negative connotation and public perception, it's frequently cited by ACA critics.

As explained above, the ACA altered the use of long-standing actuarial data to calculate premiums. The TRCP was designed to minimize risk by limiting the losses and profits for an insurer in the individual and small group markets. The TRCP encourages insurers to sell policies in these exchanges by limiting the losses, and it also prevents overpricing the uncertainty by limiting their gains.

126

If actual claims are more than 3% of estimated claims, the federal government will reimburse insurers 50% of the excess claim cost. If actual claims exceed 8%, the reimbursement rate climbs to 80%. If actual claims are less than expected, the percentages work in reverse and insurance companies pay the excess profits to the Department of Health & Humans Services (HHS). Since TRCP did not limit the reimbursements insurance companies could receive, critics labeled the TRCP as an insurance company bailout.

In response to these criticisms, Congress included language in the Consolidated and Further Continuing Appropriations Act, 2015 (H.R. 83) specifically prohibiting the HHS from using federal funds to make payments under the TRCP. According to this law, insurance companies could only be reimbursed to the extent monies were paid by other insurers for their excess profits. Although only applicable to 2015, it was intended to ensure this aspect of the ACA was budget neutral.

In early 2016, several insurance companies filed a $5 billion class action lawsuit against the United States government to receive full payment of the amounts due under the original TRCP legislation.[30] If successful, the TRCP will not be budget neutral and the HHS could be paying billions to insurance companies under the TRCP.

Use of Risk-Sharing Mechanisms

Risk sharing is not unique to the ACA. Medicare Part D and the Medicare Advantage programs use some similar risk-sharing mechanisms. The use of similar techniques for Medicare is a persuasive defense of these provisions.

Reinsurance is a common practice within the insurance industry. Insurers will assume the risk for a certain dollar amount of claims, and purchase reinsurance from another insurance company for the excess. Virtually all companies with self-insured health plans use reinsurance. Under these arrangements, the sponsoring company will pay medical claims up to a certain limit, and another insurance company will pay the excess over the threshold. Although mandated by legislation, the ACA risk-sharing provisions can be viewed as a form of reinsurance.

ACA critics have some valid concerns with the risk-sharing mechanisms. As stated, the TRCP is the most controversial and political risk-sharing mechanism of the ACA. The absence of budget neutrality and undefined termination date could cost U.S. taxpayers billions. Although the TRCP could generate revenue for the government, no one expects it will.

Critics also believe the risk-sharing mechanisms mask the true cost of insurance resulting from the ACA changes. They posit that without these provisions, insurance premiums would increase dramatically, which might further erode support for the legislation. Since the risk-sharing provisions are designed to mitigate the risks of high and disproportionate costs to insurers, their claims have merit.

Voluntary Reporting and Compliance

The revenue provisions related to the employer and individual mandates will be administered by the Internal Revenue Service (IRS), which is part of the Treasury Department. The drafters of the ACA always envisioned the IRS would be responsible for administering tax collections and any available credits, even before the Supreme Court ruled the penalties for noncompliance with the mandatory insurance provisions were a tax.[31]

There is a sound rationale for delegating the administration of the ACA tax and credit provisions to the IRS:

- The IRS is part of the Treasury Department.
- The IRS has thousands of employees who continuously interact with businesses and individuals.
- The individual tax credits are income-based.
- Collection of the individual mandate penalties can't be enforced, but any tax refunds can be confiscated.

Although it may make a lot of sense for the IRS to administer provisions of the ACA, it places an additional burden on an agency already struggling with administering a burgeoning tax code. The taxes and penalties associated with the minimum coverage and affordability requirements force tax professionals and IRS agents to understand health insurance policies in addition to the Internal Revenue Code.

The Tax Gap

The U.S. tax code and administration is based upon a system of voluntary compliance. Taxpayers are expected and required to file the appropriate forms and pay the requisite taxes due. There are fines, penalties and punishment for noncompliance. IRS auditors are trained to discover errors, omissions and fraud; however, the system is fundamentally based on taxpayers' voluntary compliance and cooperation.

A vast majority of individuals and businesses do their best to comply, but errors and omissions occur. There is also a small percentage of people who intentionally fail to pay their taxes. Their justifications range from a belief that income taxation is unconstitutional to a belief that everyone cheats on their taxes—or they're willing to play the audit lottery and hope the IRS doesn't catch them.

Underpayment of taxes is frequently referred to as the "tax gap." The IRS estimates the tax gap every few years; in 2012, the IRS estimated the 2006 tax gap to be approximately $385 billion.[32] According to the Government Accounting Office (GAO), 84% of the underpaid tax is the result of underreported income. With the IRS collecting nearly $2 trillion in taxes in 2006, the tax gap was more than 15% of the total taxes due the federal government. Congress and the IRS are continually undertaking new endeavors to close the tax gap, with little success.

**Tax Gap Components** (Dollars in billions)

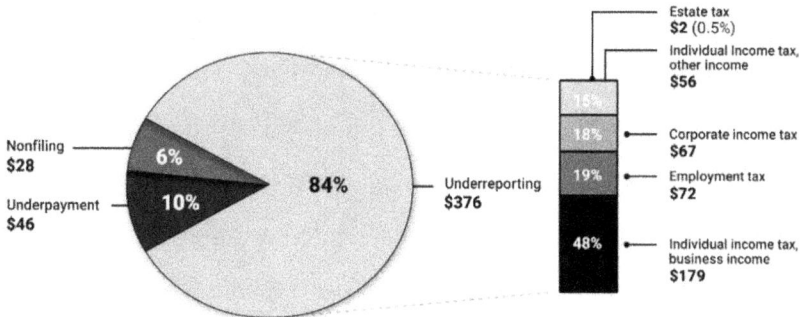

Nonfiling $28

Underpayment $46

6%

10%

84%

Underreporting $376

Estate tax $2 (0.5%)

Individual income tax, other income $56

Corporate income tax $67

Employment tax $72

Individual income tax, business income $179

15%

18%

19%

48%

Source: GAO Analysis of IRS data

The ACA has created a host of new tax provisions that can add to the tax gap:

- The individual premium tax credit,
- The individual shared responsibility payment,
- The medical device tax,
- Employer penalties for failing to offer adequate or affordable coverage, and
- Small employer tax credits.

Except for the delay of the employer mandate, most of these tax provisions were effective as of January 1, 2014. At the time of this writing, taxpayers recently filed their 2014 tax returns. Consequently, it will be a few years before the IRS and other governmental agencies can compile the statistics related to compliance with the ACA tax provisions. It's reasonable to assume errors and omissions (either accidental or intentional) related to the ACA will increase the tax gap, but it's too early to assess the magnitude.

Initial Enrollment Verification

The problems associated with the rollout of the federal and many state enrollment websites in late 2013 and early 2014 revealed a host of problems. Beyond the frequent published stories related to wait times and lost coverage, technological errors revealed the systems' deficiencies in determining eligibility, calculating advanced premium credits, and tracking enrollees who had prior insurance coverage.

Although anyone can be covered by a private insurance plan, only U.S. citizens and legal residents are allowed to enroll in an ACA health care exchange. There are millions of people living in the U.S. who are not citizens. In addition to undocumented immigrants, these individuals might be foreign nationals working for a private company, teaching, or studying at an educational institution, or simply enjoying an extended vacation. Whatever the reason, none of them are eligible to enroll in a health care exchange or receive the benefits that reduce the cost of coverage. To the extent ineligible people are enrolling in health plans and receiving tax credits or premium subsidies, the cost of their benefits were not included in the initial CBO estimates, thereby understating the ACA cost.

When people apply for insurance through a health insurance exchange, the federal or state government is supposed to verify the information submitted. Not only are they checking to make sure people obtain appropriate coverage, they are also responsible for verifying applicants' eligibility and preventing fraud by people trying to falsely claim tax credits or premium subsidies. Applications are supposed to be cross-checked against other information for validity, and any inconsistencies are flagged for follow up.

The HHS Office of Inspector General (HHS OIG) and Government Accounting Office (GAO) have conducted multiple internal investigations to determine how well the exchanges are verifying eligibility. Their findings were not reassuring.

The first HHS OIG review focused on the qualification for enrollment in qualified health plans, advanced premium tax credits and cost sharing reductions.[33] They found 2.9 million inconsistencies in applications submitted in the last quarter of 2013. As of February 23, 2014, 2.6 million (89.6%) of the inconsistencies were still unresolved. Of those 2.6 million files, nearly 45% (1.3 million) were related to citizenship and approximately one-third (965,000) were related to income. The report also discovered that four state exchanges lacked the ability to resolve inconsistencies due to "failures in their information technologies." The inability to verify either criterion could result in the payment of benefits to people not included in the CBO cost estimates.

In a separate audit the Inspector General found the internal controls for the federal exchange were ineffective in verifying Social Security numbers. [34] It also determined that the controls for California's exchange, Covered California, were not effectively identifying citizenship or lawful presence in California.

Inconsistencies don't necessarily mean the information is incorrect or fraudulent; it just can't be verified. Even if a vast majority of the inconsistencies are ultimately verified or honest mistakes, the lack of controls and inability to verify information is astounding. The weaknesses in the system are an invitation for scammers and dishonest people to exploit the system for personal gain.

Separate from the HHS OIG audits, the Government Accounting Office (GAO) conducted its own test of the exchange internal controls.[35] The GAO performed an undercover test using twelve fictitious applicants. Despite submitting phony documents, or in three cases submitting nothing, eleven bogus applicants continued to receive subsidies and premium tax credits through July 2014.

The GAO discovered that the government must rely upon insurance companies to provide information for the subsidies being paid by to the insurance companies by the government. Lacking the ability to independently verify enrollment and payment of premiums, insurance companies are likely receiving subsidies for people who are not paying their premiums.

Like the HHS OIG audits, the GAO undercover test revealed significant deficiencies in the fundamental internal controls of the exchanges. The ability to receive tax credits and premium subsidies for months after submitting false documents or no documentation is a material weakness in the system.

The IRS is charged with administering the tax credits and subsidies and should be able to resolve discrepancies related to income eligibility. However, the IRS won't be able to verify citizenship or subsidies paid to insurance companies where the eligible members didn't pay their portion of the premiums. Consequently, the inability of the state or federal exchanges to verify this information could result in persons claiming tax credits or insurance companies receiving premium subsidies to which they were not entitled, resulting in additional payments from the U.S. Treasury not allowed by the ACA or contemplated by the CBO.

## The Jury Is Out

Although most of the ACA law is in effect, some provisions have yet to be implemented or enforced. Therefore, it's impossible to render a verdict on the success or failure of the ACA. Nevertheless, there are some early indications of concern regarding the long-term fiscal implications of the ACA. Most of the waivers and delays involve revenue provisions of the ACA. The deferral of the employer mandate and non-enforcement of the individual mandate eliminates or reduces the assessment of penalties for those who don't provide or purchase the required insurance coverage.

The Republicans took control of the Senate and House of Representatives in the November 2014 elections. Although it's unlikely they will be able to fully repeal the ACA as evidenced by President Obama's veto of Restoring Americans' Healthcare Freedom Reconciliation Act of 2015, Congress did halt the collection of the medical device tax for two years as part of the Consolidated Appropriations act of 2016. The repeal of the tax may be good economic policy, but if repealed, it will reduce projected ACA revenues by $30 billion over ten years.[36]

As with most financial issues, our national leaders are not very forthcoming with accurate and understandable information, and the ACA is no different. Expect proponents to proclaim its success and opponents to declare its failure. This chapter directs you to the areas to monitor as future reports regarding the financial implications of the ACA are made available.

Although the ultimate budgetary impact of the ACA won't be known for years, or even decades, it seems highly questionable at this time the ACA will be budget neutral. Since it's too early to assess the financial success of the ACA, this chapter highlights some future financial risks associated with the legislation. Considering the U.S. spends over $3 trillion on health care services, there is significant risk to the U.S. taxpayers if the CBO projections of budget neutrality are incorrect. If the ACA ultimately adds to the annual deficit, the cost may be worth the other objectives and benefits of the ACA, but that's a decision ultimately decided by the American electorate, best made with accurate information.

# CHAPTER 7
# THE FUTURE

<hr>

Predicting the Future

One thing is certain: no one knows the future. Those who offer prognostications will undoubtedly be wrong. Even the experts and people with intimate knowledge about certain topics are frequently surprised by events. Consider these significant events in American history:

- The American government was negotiating with Japan when the Japanese military attacked Pearl Harbor.

- None of the national security agencies or personnel predicted or prevented the attacks of September 11, 2001.

- There were many bright people on Wall Street who were surprised by the collapse of the financial markets in September 2008 and the bankruptcy of Lehman Brothers.

The point . . . be leery of anyone who tries to predict the future, good or bad.

Even though we can't predict future events, we can use common sense and wisdom to recognize that certain behaviors or decisions will ultimately lead to damaging consequences. Consider the addiction analogy in the Debt chapter. You may not be able to specifically predict the consequences an addict will suffer, but common sense tells you that an alcoholic or drug addict will eventually wreak havoc in his or her own life and the lives of others. The same can be said of current U.S. fiscal policy. We may not be able to adequately predict the consequence of continuous deficits and growing debt, but do you honestly believe this can continue indefinitely without consequence? After reading this book, I certainly hope not.

We must only look around the world to see examples of what happens to countries with unsustainable debt and spending. Developing countries have faced financial crisis, runaway inflation, and currency collapses for decades. Recently, developed nations have started facing these same issues. Since 2008, multiple Western European countries have encountered some degree of financial crisis, with Greece experiencing the most severe and recurring problems.

There are many aspects and nuances to Greece's problems, but in short, the government has been spending at an unsustainable pace. Since 2009, Greek leaders have agreed to certain reform and austerity measures intended to stem excess spending in exchange for additional extensions of credit. Despite the promises and expectations, nothing really changed. In 2015, the Greek people decided they were tired of the austerity measures and elected government leaders who promised to roll back austerity and increase government spending. Greece discovered a fundamental flaw in their plan; the lenders didn't agree.

When faced with a similar situation in 2012, the European Central Bank (ECB) and other European leaders panicked over Greece's potential exit from the Eurozone and were willing to compromise and continue lending money to keep Greece in the European Union. This was no longer the case in 2015. European politicians and bankers demanded specific measures in exchange for more lending. At first, Greece balked. However, after more than a week of banks being closed, depositors being limited to withdrawing a maximum of 60 euros per day and a looming financial collapse, Greece capitulated to the demands of its creditors.

The Greek government and people learned a very difficult and invaluable lesson in this process. You can't demand or force lenders to give you more money on your terms. They also realized the more you need someone else's money, the more you must surrender to their requirements. The Book of Proverbs is referred to as a Biblical book of wisdom, and most of the sayings are attributable to King Solomon. Proverbs 7:6 states, "A borrower is servant to the lender." This was a hard lesson the Greek people learned, and something U.S. citizens should remember.

A financial crisis in the U.S. will be different from the one in Greece, but in some manner, we will be forced to submit to the demands of our creditors. Just like you as an individual, a business enterprise, or a country like Greece, the more the U.S. becomes indebted to others, the more our nation becomes a servant to those lenders. Additionally, the more we need their money, the more power and influence they will exercise over our decisions.

The Greek people discovered that if they are unable to make the necessary decisions to stop excessive spending and borrowing, eventually someone else will make those decisions for them. Fortunately for us, we're not in that position . . . yet. We still have the power to control our own decisions and destiny, but we may surrender that power unless we get serious about balancing the budget and reducing the debt.

<u>Finding Solutions</u>

Providing simple, commonsense explanations of the United States deficit and debt is the purpose of this book. For multiple reasons, this book was never intended to offer potential solutions. Instead, the intention was to educate and increase your awareness of the issues.

As previously stated, there are no easy solutions to the problems we face. If it were easy, it would have already been done. The task may be daunting, but it's achievable. As with any solution, you first have to identity the problem or objective. One of the greatest challenges we face as a nation in solving our fiscal issues is the lack of understandable information. Hopefully, *A Sinking Nation* has increased your awareness and knowledge and has equipped you to engage in conversations of the issues and potential solutions.

Beyond the commonsense financial principles discussed in the previous chapters, I believe any proposal to balance the budget and reduce the debt must contain four essential components.

1.  Political compromise

2.  Sacrifice

3.  Spending and taxes

4.  Immediate change

Political compromise. It's difficult to determine if Washington reflects the nation, or if the nation is a reflection of Washington. Whichever it is, the political climate of America is polarized and contentious. There is a lot of animosity and distrust going in all directions. Unfortunately, such an environment makes it extremely difficult to forge some type of agreement to address our nation's fiscal issues.

The financial state of the country demands solutions which transcend any one person or group. There are far too many interested parties and stakeholders for one person or group to adequately craft all of the solutions. In the end, it's going to require people from all walks of life coming together with an attitude and expectation of working together to find solutions.

The current political climate has practically eliminated compromise from political discourse. It may be appropriate to refuse compromise on certain moral issues, but in my opinion, spending and tax policies are fundamentally economic issues, not moral ones. On most matters, our elected officials refuse to compromise for political reasons. They're afraid compromise will embolden another person or party, which will make it more difficult for them to gain or retain power. Given the problems we face, our leaders must be willing to compromise, and those who refuse should be voted out of office.

Sacrifice. Sacrifice is not a very popular word in modern American culture. Without doubt, there are very brave men and women who sacrifice every day defending our nation, responding to people in need, and taking care of their families, friends and communities. However, it seems like there has been an overall shift in the American mindset and attitude, especially when it comes to the government.

Entitlement programs speak for themselves. The government defines them as programs whose benefits you are entitled to as long as you meet certain criteria. Whether intentional or not, this terminology has contributed to an attitude among the American people that they are entitled to receive those benefits. The entitlement mentality is not limited just to those people who receive benefits specifically classified as entitlement programs (i.e., food assistance and welfare). People of all socio-economic classes have come to expect the government to provide certain things for them. An entitlement mentality focuses on what someone is going to provide for you, but it ignores the other half of the equation: someone else is obligated to provide whatever you're entitled to receive.

This entitlement attitude is pervasive across the U.S. Think of the number of building and construction projects which have been approved because it only costs local taxpayers a small percentage of the total cost, and the majority of the cost is paid by the federal government. Somehow, federal grants are treated like magical money, as if it appears out of nothing. There is no free money. Any money doled out by the government was received or borrowed from someone else.

NIMBY (Not in My Back Yard) references local opposition to certain construction projects. As an example, we all recognize the need for landfills and sewage treatment plants. We just don't want them built near our property (i.e., not in my back yard). While opposition to such projects is understandable, this attitude effectively results in a transfer of the burden to someone else. The same attitude often surfaces when addressing the fiscal challenges of the nation.

Most of the American populace supports balancing the budget and reducing the debt. Conceptually, it's easy to support higher taxes, reduced spending, or both. We don't mind higher taxes, provided someone else is paying, and we're all for reduced spending, as long as the money we receive isn't reduced. These attitudes are the crux of the problem. We want to balance the budget and reduce the debt, but we don't want it to cost us anything. However, we all must be willing to pay more and receive less in order for us to succeed.

What are you willing to sacrifice to secure the financial security of our nation? Are you willing to pay more in taxes? Are you willing to reduce or defer your Social Security benefits? Are you willing to eliminate or curtail certain programs? None of your ideas may get enacted, but it has to start with people willing to give up something. If someone is not willing to personally sacrifice in some measure, then I question how serious they are about addressing the problem. Once again the time has come to answer the famous question posed by President John F. Kennedy, "Ask not what your country can do for you. Ask what you can do for your country."

Spending and taxes. The perpetual fight in Washington involves spending and taxes. One group believes our problems can be solved by cutting spending, and another believes we just have to raise more taxes. The Deficit chapter explained why both of these precepts are flawed presuppositions. In reality, an effective solution is going to involve spending cuts and tax increases.

To the chagrin of many people inside and outside of Washington, any viable solution must include reforming mandatory spending (i.e., entitlement programs). Although this may seem like a contradiction to my stated goal of not offering specific solutions, acknowledging the necessity of entitlement reform is a practical reality. The specific solutions will dictate how the reductions will be implemented.

To recognize this practical reality, simply review the allocation of federal spending. Entitlement programs currently consume more than 60% of all federal spending, and are expected to grow in the coming decades. By simple math, there is not enough money in the rest of the budget to achieve the necessary savings. It's analogous to a family making $60,000 and spending $75,000 per year, of which more than $45,000 is for their mortgage and taxes. Although it's helpful to cut their cable bill by $100 per month, it's not going to fix their financial woes. The real problem is spending more than 60% of their income for their house, and reducing their housing costs is the most likely path to balancing their budget. The numbers are exponentially larger, but the same concept applies to entitlement spending and the U.S. budget.

A similar argument can be made for raising taxes. There may be economic arguments for lower taxes, but it's highly unlikely a workable solution will be reached without some increase in taxes. Part of this assessment is an acknowledgement of the political landscape. Without a dramatic shift in the balance of power in Washington, which doesn't seem likely in the near future, achieving a balanced budget only through spending cuts is not likely to pass Congress even if Republicans control the White House, Senate and House of Representatives. Since entitlement and other programs tend to impact people on the lower social-economic strata, it's inequitable to balance the budget solely through spending cuts.

It may shock some people, but a number of my wealthy clients would embrace an increase in taxes if the additional revenues were specifically dedicated to debt reduction. A number of my colleagues have expressed similar sentiments from their wealthy clients. Many of them are very skeptical Congress would use the additional revenues to reduce the debt and would divert the additional funds to support increased spending. This may seem like a cynical attitude, but the Congressional track record has proven their skepticism is well-deserved. Like all issues of trust, there are no easy ways for Congress to regain the confidence of the American people, but it probably starts with small measures of compromise and follow through.

Immediate results. In my opinion, one of the ways you will be able to measure how serious our leaders are in tackling this problem is their willingness to enact immediate spending cuts. As outlined in the chapter on the Deficit, Congress measures revenues and spending over a 10-year horizon, and spending cuts are often deferred until the latter years. With this approach, politicians can claim they cut spending, but in reality they are deferring the difficult decisions to another day and postponing any potential voter backlash. There is greater political risk in voting for spending cuts that affect your current constituents, knowing it might cost you votes in the next election.

I think a politician is serious about tackling the debt and deficit if he or she is willing to offend special interest groups within their constituency and potentially lose their next election by reducing or eliminating certain federal benefits. In contrast, I question their commitment to balancing the budget and paying down the debt if they want to kick the can down the road or transfer the negative impact to another constituency.

Since I previously stated that a sound proposal should include tax increases along with spending cuts, it may seem imbalanced to focus only on immediate spending cuts. While the principle of immediate results does apply to revenue increases and spending cuts equally, rarely does legislation defer tax increases until late in the 10-year horizon while enacting spending cuts immediately. Since it is much more likely Congress will attempt to defer spending cuts, any proposal must be carefully scrutinized to determine when the cuts occur, or how long it's going to take before a balanced budget is achieved.

## Go Big or Start Small

Go big or go home is a modern cliché. The message communicates a willingness to take great risks, which might result in tremendous failure. It follows the line of thinking that it's better to attempt something big and fail, then play it safe and succeed.

Since the 2011 battle between President Obama and Republican Congressional leaders over raising the debt ceiling, there have been discussions about a grand bargain that will raise taxes and cut spending to balance the budget and stop increasing the national debt. Unfortunately, the grand bargain has never materialized. The inability to agree to some big deal has resulted in maintaining the status quo, with a promise to revisit the matter after the next election.

Although it will take big changes to regain the financial security of our nation, it doesn't have to be an all-or-nothing proposition. If Congress and the President can't reach some grand bargain, they should pass smaller incremental legislation that will reduce the annual deficits. To quote Lao Tzu, "A journey of a thousand miles begins with a single step." It may be a long journey to balance the budget and eliminate the $19 trillion debt, but a small compromise can be the initial step.

It's like the example of the family with the big house cited earlier in the chapter. Cutting their cable bill isn't going to solve their problem, but it's a first step. More importantly, it is an action they can implement immediately. If the best solution required selling their house, the process of selling a home and finding a new residence could take weeks or months. Big changes take time, but small savings can be implemented immediately. Savings from small changes like reducing a utility bill follows a basic financial principle that small amounts of money add up over time, especially when the power of compounding is applied.

The same principle applies to the U.S. government. Although a grand bargain is probably necessary, the inability to strike a big deal is no excuse for inaction. Small deals may not fix the problem, but they can start the process. Hopefully, minor compromises will build trust and goodwill amongst the parties and voters, which will lead to more significant reforms. Furthermore, small savings are still savings and will reduce future spending cuts or additional revenues needed to completely fix the problem.

## A Time For Action

We are not facing an immediate financial crisis, but we're moving closer to one each day. Consider just a few points from the prior chapters.

- The current annual budget deficit has dropped dramatically from the $1.09 trillion deficit in Fiscal 2012. However, annual deficits are expected to rise over the next few years and at no time in the future is the U.S. government projected to spend less than it collects.

- The national debt has topped $19 trillion and will be fast approaching $20 trillion by the time the next President takes office.

- The Social Security Disability Trust Fund is facing a solvency crisis and Social Security is currently paying out more in benefits than it receives each year, causing it to cash in on the IOUs from the general funds of the Treasury.

Each of the facts listed above is a significant financial challenge, in and of itself. Combined, they present a fairly bleak outlook. If we don't want to end up in a financial crisis like some of our European allies, we need to act now. As previously stated, the sooner we tackle the problems, the more options we have. As Greece learned in 2015, when no one will lend you money, you have to accept the terms of those who will. We don't want to be in a similar situation.

<u>What Next?</u>

Having read this far, it should be clear the financial security of our nation is at risk, and unfortunately, the dysfunctional political environment in Washington doesn't offer much hope anything will change soon. The situation is very frustrating and can seem hopeless at times, but now is not the time for anyone who's concerned about these issues to wave the white flag of surrender. Rather, now is the time to engage our family, friends, community and political leaders to fix the financial mess we now face.

So what can you do? The following are a few suggestions.

- Stay informed. The economic and political environments are constantly changing and shifting. Beyond trustworthy news and media outlets, there are a number of sources and resources discussing this topic. DebtandDeficit.com is connected with this book and will continue to provide information and analysis of pertinent issues and legislation.

- Ask questions. Hopefully, after reading *A Sinking Nation* you have a much better understanding of the issues and can ask questions (and follow-up questions) in a manner that will be much more difficult for politicians and pundits to spin or evade.

- Vote. Vote for those candidates who have positions and policies which indicate they are serious about addressing our fiscal challenges. It's easy for politicians to say they want to balance the budget and reduce the national debt, but you must confirm their policies and votes are consistent with their rhetoric. Politicians are notorious for acting differently once they're voted into office. If your elected representative doesn't uphold his or her word, support a different candidate during the next election. In the words of President Ronald Reagan, "Trust but verify."

- Personal contribution. How are you willing to contribute to balancing the budget and cutting the debt? It might be paying a little more in taxes, accepting reduced Social Security or other government benefits, or something else. If you're serious about solving the problem, you have to be willing to make some sacrifice towards securing our financial future. In the end it may not cost you much, but you have to be willing to pay something. The situation affects us all, so we all need to be part of the solution, and if you're not willing to sacrifice something, how can you expect someone else?

There are a host of other ways for you to get engaged in the discussion and process of changing our current trajectory, but these are a few simple things everyone can do.

Conclusion

As described throughout this book, the financial security and future of our nation is grim. For decades, the federal government has overspent and continued to borrow money to pay for its deficit spending. The highly dysfunctional political environment currently overshadowing Washington DC doesn't bode well for reaching any meaningful solutions in the near term. All of this can be very discouraging and make the situation seem hopeless.

One of the greatest challenges you may face is to believe that it's possible to correct our financial woes, or that your efforts can make a difference. As bleak as the outlook might be, it's not too late. There is still time to balance the budget and put us on a path to paying down the national debt. It won't be easy to break old habits and form new ones, but it can be done. History has proven our nation can rise to the occasion and resolve challenging issues (e.g., eliminating slavery, women's suffrage, helping to win World War II, and the civil rights movement). There may have been a few major personalities we associate with each of these transformative issues, but in reality, success was achieved by scores of individuals sacrificing in small ways. It will be the same for addressing the deficit and debt.

Let's join together and we can break the habit of perpetual deficit spending that is slowly sinking our nation.

# KEY QUESTIONS

There are a multitude of questions you can ask elected officials and candidates to evaluate their positions, policies, and proposals regarding the fiscal affairs of the U.S. government. The following are a few queries to consider when discussing these topics; you might also listen carefully to the answers provided by officials and candidates keeping these questions in mind.

## The Deficit

- Should the U.S. government balance the annual budget?
- How long should it take to achieve a balanced federal budget?
- What spending cuts do you support?
- What tax increases do you support?
- Should Congress pass separate appropriation bills instead of passing omnibus spending bills?

## The Debt

- Is the national debt a threat to the fiscal stability of the U.S.?
- What are the financial indicators the national debt has become unsustainable?
- What are the implications of increased interest rates?
- Who is funding the increases in the national debt?
- Should there be a ceiling on the federal debt?

Social Security

- Do you support changing the current eligibility criteria for retirement benefits?
- What are the assets held by the Social Security Trust Fund?
- What happened to the excess funds collected for Social Security?
- How are the funds going to be generated to repay the Trust Fund loans?
- What changes are necessary to increase the solvency of the Disability Fund?

Affordable Care Act

- How many people currently have health insurance who did not have health insurance before the implementation of the ACA?
- For those who obtained coverage from the ACA, how many are receiving coverage from Medicaid and how many from private insurance?
- How is the ACA "bending the cost curve" of health insurance premiums and health care services?
- What are the financial measures that will determine if the ACA is budget neutral, provides a surplus, or operates in a deficit?
- How have the delays and changes impacted the budget neutrality of the ACA?

# TABLES

## TABLE 1

### SURPLUSES OR (DEFICITS)
### BY FUND GROUP: 1934 – 1974
(in millions)

| Fiscal Year | Surplus or (Deficit) | | |
| | Total | Federal Funds | Trust Funds |
|---|---|---|---|
| 1934 | (3,586) | (3,633) | 47 |
| 1935 | (2,803) | (2,849) | 46 |
| 1936 | (4,304) | (4,464) | 159 |
| 1937 | (2,193) | (2,826) | 633 |
| 1938 | (89) | (1,212) | 1,124 |
| 1939 | (2,846) | (3,896) | 1,051 |
| 1940 | (2,920) | (4,045) | 1,125 |
| 1941 | (4,941) | (6,360) | 1,419 |
| 1942 | (20,503) | (22,496) | 1,992 |
| 1943 | (54,554) | (57,648) | 3,094 |
| 1944 | (47,557) | (51,818) | 4,261 |
| 1945 | (47,553) | (52,972) | 5,419 |
| 1946 | (15,936) | (19,847) | 3,910 |
| 1947 | 4,018 | 577 | 3,441 |
| 1948 | 11,796 | 8,834 | 2,962 |
| 1949 | 580 | (1,838) | 2,417 |
| 1950 | (3,119) | (3,055) | (65) |
| 1951 | 6,102 | 2,451 | 3,651 |
| 1952 | (1,519) | (5,005) | 3,486 |
| 1953 | (6,493) | (9,921) | 3,427 |
| 1954 | (1,154) | (3,151) | 1,997 |
| 1955 | (2,993) | (4,173) | 1,180 |
| 1956 | 3,947 | 1,313 | 2,634 |
| 1957 | 3,412 | 1,657 | 1,755 |
| 1958 | (2,769) | (3,017) | 248 |
| 1959 | (12,849) | (11,271) | (1,578) |
| 1960 | 301 | 791 | (490) |
| 1961 | (3,335) | (4,193) | 858 |
| 1962 | (7,146) | (6,847) | (299) |
| 1963 | (4,756) | (6,630) | 1,874 |
| 1964 | (5,915) | (8,588) | 2,673 |
| 1965 | (1,411) | (3,910) | 2,499 |
| 1966 | (3,698) | (5,165) | 1,467 |
| 1967 | (8,643) | (15,709) | 7,066 |
| 1968 | (25,161) | (28,373) | 3,212 |
| 1969 | 3,242 | (4,871) | 8,112 |
| 1970 | (2,842) | (13,168) | 10,326 |
| 1971 | (23,033) | (29,896) | 6,863 |
| 1972 | (23,373) | (29,296) | 5,924 |
| 1973 | (14,908) | (25,683) | 10,774 |
| 1974 | (6,135) | (20,144) | 14,009 |

Source:    http://www.whitehouse.gov/omb/budget/Historicals/

## TABLE 1

### SURPLUSES OR (DEFICITS)
### BY FUND GROUP: 1975 – 2015
(in millions)

| Fiscal Year | Surplus or (Deficit) | | |
| | Total | Federal Funds | Trust Funds |
|---|---|---|---|
| 1975 | (53,242) | (60,664) | 7,422 |
| 1976 | (73,732) | (76,138) | 2,405 |
| 1977 | (53,659) | (63,155) | 9,495 |
| 1978 | (59,185) | (71,876) | 12,691 |
| 1979 | (40,726) | (59,061) | 18,335 |
| 1980 | (73,830) | (82,632) | 8,802 |
| 1981 | (78,968) | (85,791) | 6,823 |
| 1982 | (127,977) | (134,221) | 6,244 |
| 1983 | (207,802) | (230,874) | 23,072 |
| 1984 | (185,367) | (218,272) | 32,905 |
| 1985 | (212,308) | (266,457) | 54,149 |
| 1986 | (221,227) | (283,120) | 61,893 |
| 1987 | (149,730) | (222,348) | 72,618 |
| 1988 | (155,178) | (252,902) | 97,724 |
| 1989 | (152,639) | (276,122) | 123,483 |
| 1990 | (221,036) | (341,181) | 120,145 |
| 1991 | (269,238) | (380,971) | 111,733 |
| 1992 | (290,321) | (386,338) | 96,018 |
| 1993 | (255,051) | (355,436) | 100,385 |
| 1994 | (203,186) | (298,508) | 95,322 |
| 1995 | (163,952) | (263,211) | 99,259 |
| 1996 | (107,431) | (222,052) | 114,621 |
| 1997 | (21,884) | (147,826) | 125,942 |
| 1998 | 69,270 | (91,927) | 161,197 |
| 1999 | 125,610 | (87,120) | 212,730 |
| 2000 | 236,241 | 1,629 | 234,612 |
| 2001 | 128,236 | (100,513) | 228,749 |
| 2002 | (157,758) | (360,156) | 202,398 |
| 2003 | (377,585) | (555,977) | 178,392 |
| 2004 | (412,727) | (605,365) | 192,638 |
| 2005 | (318,346) | (555,093) | 236,747 |
| 2006 | (248,181) | (537,271) | 289,090 |
| 2007 | (160,701) | (409,395) | 248,694 |
| 2008 | (458,553) | (724,621) | 266,068 |
| 2009 | (1,412,688) | (1,539,978) | 127,290 |
| 2010 | (1,293,489) | (1,416,821) | 123,332 |
| 2011 | (1,299,595) | (1,396,642) | 97,047 |
| 2012 | (1,086,963) | (1,176,827) | 89,864 |
| 2013 | (679,544) | (765,931) | 86,387 |
| 2014 | (484,627) | (613,175) | 128,548 |
| 2015 | (438,406) | (549,975) | 111,569 |

Source:    http://www.whitehouse.gov/omb/budget/Historicals/

## TABLE 2

### RECEIPTS BY SOURCE: 1934 – 1974

(in millions)

| Fiscal Year | Individual Income Taxes | % | Corporate Income Taxes | % | Social Insurance | % | Excise Taxes | % | Other | % | Total Receipts |
|---|---|---|---|---|---|---|---|---|---|---|---|
| 1934 | 420 | 14% | 364 | 12% | 30 | 1% | 1,354 | 46% | 788 | 27% | 2,955 |
| 1935 | 527 | 15% | 529 | 15% | 31 | 1% | 1,439 | 40% | 1,084 | 30% | 3,609 |
| 1936 | 674 | 17% | 719 | 18% | 52 | 1% | 1,631 | 42% | 847 | 22% | 3,923 |
| 1937 | 1,092 | 20% | 1,038 | 19% | 580 | 11% | 1,876 | 35% | 801 | 15% | 5,387 |
| 1938 | 1,286 | 19% | 1,287 | 19% | 1,541 | 23% | 1,863 | 28% | 773 | 11% | 6,751 |
| 1939 | 1,029 | 16% | 1,127 | 18% | 1,593 | 25% | 1,871 | 30% | 675 | 11% | 6,295 |
| 1940 | 892 | 14% | 1,197 | 18% | 1,785 | 27% | 1,977 | 30% | 698 | 11% | 6,548 |
| 1941 | 1,314 | 15% | 2,124 | 24% | 1,940 | 22% | 2,552 | 29% | 781 | 9% | 8,712 |
| 1942 | 3,263 | 22% | 4,719 | 32% | 2,452 | 17% | 3,399 | 23% | 801 | 5% | 14,634 |
| 1943 | 6,505 | 27% | 9,557 | 40% | 3,044 | 13% | 4,096 | 17% | 800 | 3% | 24,001 |
| 1944 | 19,705 | 45% | 14,838 | 34% | 3,473 | 8% | 4,759 | 11% | 972 | 2% | 43,747 |
| 1945 | 18,372 | 41% | 15,988 | 35% | 3,451 | 8% | 6,265 | 14% | 1,083 | 2% | 45,159 |
| 1946 | 16,098 | 41% | 11,883 | 30% | 3,115 | 8% | 6,998 | 18% | 1,202 | 3% | 39,296 |
| 1947 | 17,935 | 47% | 8,615 | 22% | 3,422 | 9% | 7,211 | 19% | 1,331 | 3% | 38,514 |
| 1948 | 19,315 | 46% | 9,678 | 23% | 3,751 | 9% | 7,356 | 18% | 1,461 | 4% | 41,560 |
| 1949 | 15,552 | 39% | 11,192 | 28% | 3,781 | 10% | 7,502 | 19% | 1,388 | 4% | 39,415 |
| 1950 | 15,755 | 40% | 10,449 | 26% | 4,338 | 11% | 7,550 | 19% | 1,351 | 3% | 39,443 |
| 1951 | 21,616 | 42% | 14,101 | 27% | 5,674 | 11% | 8,648 | 17% | 1,578 | 3% | 51,616 |
| 1952 | 27,934 | 42% | 21,226 | 32% | 6,445 | 10% | 8,852 | 13% | 1,710 | 3% | 66,167 |
| 1953 | 29,816 | 43% | 21,238 | 31% | 6,820 | 10% | 9,877 | 14% | 1,857 | 3% | 69,608 |
| 1954 | 29,542 | 42% | 21,101 | 30% | 7,208 | 10% | 9,945 | 14% | 1,905 | 3% | 69,701 |
| 1955 | 28,747 | 44% | 17,861 | 27% | 7,862 | 12% | 9,131 | 14% | 1,850 | 3% | 65,451 |
| 1956 | 32,188 | 43% | 20,880 | 28% | 9,320 | 12% | 9,929 | 13% | 2,270 | 3% | 74,587 |
| 1957 | 35,620 | 45% | 21,167 | 26% | 9,997 | 12% | 10,534 | 13% | 2,672 | 3% | 79,990 |
| 1958 | 34,724 | 44% | 20,074 | 25% | 11,239 | 14% | 10,638 | 13% | 2,961 | 4% | 79,636 |
| 1959 | 36,719 | 46% | 17,309 | 22% | 11,722 | 15% | 10,578 | 13% | 2,921 | 4% | 79,249 |
| 1960 | 40,715 | 44% | 21,494 | 23% | 14,683 | 16% | 11,676 | 13% | 3,923 | 4% | 92,492 |
| 1961 | 41,338 | 44% | 20,954 | 22% | 16,439 | 17% | 11,860 | 13% | 3,796 | 4% | 94,388 |
| 1962 | 45,571 | 46% | 20,523 | 21% | 17,046 | 17% | 12,534 | 13% | 4,001 | 4% | 99,676 |
| 1963 | 47,588 | 45% | 21,579 | 20% | 19,804 | 19% | 13,194 | 12% | 4,395 | 4% | 106,560 |
| 1964 | 48,697 | 43% | 23,493 | 21% | 21,963 | 20% | 13,731 | 12% | 4,731 | 4% | 112,613 |
| 1965 | 48,792 | 42% | 25,461 | 22% | 22,242 | 19% | 14,570 | 12% | 5,753 | 5% | 116,817 |
| 1966 | 55,446 | 42% | 30,073 | 23% | 25,546 | 20% | 13,062 | 10% | 6,708 | 5% | 130,835 |
| 1967 | 61,526 | 41% | 33,971 | 23% | 32,619 | 22% | 13,719 | 9% | 6,987 | 5% | 148,822 |
| 1968 | 68,726 | 45% | 28,665 | 19% | 33,923 | 22% | 14,079 | 9% | 7,580 | 5% | 152,973 |
| 1969 | 87,249 | 47% | 36,678 | 20% | 39,015 | 21% | 15,222 | 8% | 8,718 | 5% | 186,882 |
| 1970 | 90,412 | 47% | 32,829 | 17% | 44,362 | 23% | 15,705 | 8% | 9,499 | 5% | 192,807 |
| 1971 | 86,230 | 46% | 26,785 | 14% | 47,325 | 25% | 16,614 | 9% | 10,185 | 5% | 187,139 |
| 1972 | 94,737 | 46% | 32,166 | 16% | 52,574 | 25% | 15,477 | 7% | 12,355 | 6% | 207,309 |
| 1973 | 103,246 | 45% | 36,153 | 16% | 63,115 | 27% | 16,260 | 7% | 12,026 | 5% | 230,799 |
| 1974 | 118,952 | 45% | 38,620 | 15% | 75,071 | 29% | 16,844 | 6% | 13,737 | 5% | 263,224 |

Source: http://www.whitehouse.gov/omb/budget/Historicals/

## TABLE 2

### RECEIPTS BY SOURCE: 1975 – 2015

(in millions)

| Fiscal Year | Individual Income Taxes | % | Corporate Income Taxes | % | Social Insurance | % | Excise Taxes | % | Other | % | Total Receipts |
|---|---|---|---|---|---|---|---|---|---|---|---|
| 1975 | 122,386 | 44% | 40,621 | 15% | 84,534 | 30% | 16,551 | 6% | 14,998 | 5% | 279,090 |
| 1976 | 131,603 | 44% | 41,409 | 14% | 90,769 | 30% | 16,963 | 6% | 17,317 | 6% | 298,060 |
| 1977 | 157,626 | 44% | 54,892 | 15% | 106,485 | 30% | 17,548 | 5% | 19,008 | 5% | 355,559 |
| 1978 | 180,988 | 45% | 59,952 | 15% | 120,967 | 30% | 18,376 | 5% | 19,278 | 5% | 399,561 |
| 1979 | 217,841 | 47% | 65,677 | 14% | 138,939 | 30% | 18,745 | 4% | 22,101 | 5% | 463,302 |
| 1980 | 244,069 | 47% | 64,600 | 12% | 157,803 | 31% | 24,329 | 5% | 26,311 | 5% | 517,112 |
| 1981 | 285,917 | 48% | 61,137 | 10% | 182,720 | 30% | 40,839 | 7% | 28,659 | 5% | 599,272 |
| 1982 | 297,744 | 48% | 49,207 | 8% | 201,498 | 33% | 36,311 | 6% | 33,006 | 5% | 617,766 |
| 1983 | 288,938 | 48% | 37,022 | 6% | 208,994 | 35% | 35,300 | 6% | 30,309 | 5% | 600,562 |
| 1984 | 298,415 | 45% | 56,893 | 9% | 239,376 | 36% | 37,361 | 6% | 34,392 | 5% | 666,438 |
| 1985 | 334,531 | 46% | 61,331 | 8% | 265,163 | 36% | 35,992 | 5% | 37,020 | 5% | 734,037 |
| 1986 | 348,959 | 45% | 63,143 | 8% | 283,901 | 37% | 32,919 | 4% | 40,233 | 5% | 769,155 |
| 1987 | 392,557 | 46% | 83,926 | 10% | 303,318 | 36% | 32,457 | 4% | 42,029 | 5% | 854,288 |
| 1988 | 401,181 | 44% | 94,508 | 10% | 334,335 | 37% | 35,227 | 4% | 43,987 | 5% | 909,238 |
| 1989 | 445,690 | 45% | 103,291 | 10% | 359,416 | 36% | 34,386 | 3% | 48,321 | 5% | 991,105 |
| 1990 | 466,884 | 45% | 93,507 | 9% | 380,047 | 37% | 35,345 | 3% | 56,174 | 5% | 1,031,958 |
| 1991 | 467,827 | 44% | 98,086 | 9% | 396,016 | 38% | 42,402 | 4% | 50,657 | 5% | 1,054,988 |
| 1992 | 475,964 | 44% | 100,270 | 9% | 413,689 | 38% | 45,569 | 4% | 55,717 | 5% | 1,091,208 |
| 1993 | 509,680 | 44% | 117,520 | 10% | 428,300 | 37% | 48,057 | 4% | 50,778 | 4% | 1,154,335 |
| 1994 | 543,055 | 43% | 140,385 | 11% | 461,475 | 37% | 55,225 | 4% | 58,427 | 5% | 1,258,566 |
| 1995 | 590,244 | 44% | 157,004 | 12% | 484,473 | 36% | 57,484 | 4% | 62,585 | 5% | 1,351,790 |
| 1996 | 656,417 | 45% | 171,824 | 12% | 509,414 | 35% | 54,014 | 4% | 61,384 | 4% | 1,453,053 |
| 1997 | 737,466 | 47% | 182,293 | 12% | 539,371 | 34% | 56,924 | 4% | 63,178 | 4% | 1,579,232 |
| 1998 | 828,586 | 48% | 188,677 | 11% | 571,831 | 33% | 57,673 | 3% | 74,961 | 4% | 1,721,728 |
| 1999 | 879,480 | 48% | 184,680 | 10% | 611,833 | 33% | 70,414 | 4% | 81,045 | 4% | 1,827,452 |
| 2000 | 1,004,462 | 50% | 207,289 | 10% | 652,852 | 32% | 68,865 | 3% | 91,723 | 5% | 2,025,191 |
| 2001 | 994,339 | 50% | 151,075 | 8% | 693,967 | 35% | 66,232 | 3% | 85,169 | 4% | 1,991,082 |
| 2002 | 858,345 | 46% | 148,044 | 8% | 700,760 | 38% | 66,989 | 4% | 78,998 | 4% | 1,853,136 |
| 2003 | 793,699 | 45% | 131,778 | 7% | 712,978 | 40% | 67,524 | 4% | 76,335 | 4% | 1,782,314 |
| 2004 | 808,959 | 43% | 189,371 | 10% | 733,407 | 39% | 69,855 | 4% | 78,522 | 4% | 1,880,114 |
| 2005 | 927,222 | 43% | 278,282 | 13% | 794,125 | 37% | 73,094 | 3% | 80,888 | 4% | 2,153,611 |
| 2006 | 1,043,908 | 43% | 353,915 | 15% | 837,821 | 35% | 73,961 | 3% | 97,264 | 4% | 2,406,869 |
| 2007 | 1,163,472 | 45% | 370,243 | 14% | 869,607 | 34% | 65,069 | 3% | 99,594 | 4% | 2,567,985 |
| 2008 | 1,145,747 | 45% | 304,346 | 12% | 900,155 | 36% | 67,334 | 3% | 106,409 | 4% | 2,523,991 |
| 2009 | 915,308 | 43% | 138,229 | 7% | 890,917 | 42% | 62,483 | 3% | 98,052 | 5% | 2,104,989 |
| 2010 | 898,549 | 42% | 191,437 | 9% | 864,814 | 40% | 66,909 | 3% | 141,015 | 7% | 2,162,724 |
| 2011 | 1,091,473 | 47% | 181,085 | 8% | 818,792 | 36% | 72,381 | 3% | 139,735 | 6% | 2,303,466 |
| 2012 | 1,132,206 | 46% | 242,289 | 10% | 845,314 | 35% | 79,061 | 3% | 151,118 | 6% | 2,449,988 |
| 2013 | 1,316,405 | 47% | 273,506 | 10% | 947,820 | 34% | 84,007 | 3% | 153,365 | 6% | 2,775,103 |
| 2014 | 1,394,568 | 46% | 320,731 | 11% | 1,023,458 | 34% | 93,368 | 3% | 189,362 | 6% | 3,021,487 |
| 2015 | 1,540,802 | 47% | 343,797 | 11% | 1,065,257 | 33% | 98,279 | 3% | 201,751 | 6% | 3,249,886 |

Source: http://www.whitehouse.gov/omb/budget/Historicals/

| TABLE 3 | TABLE 3 |
|---|---|
| **SURPLUSES OR (DEFICITS) AS A PERCENTAGE OF GDP 1934 – 1974** (in billions) | **SURPLUSES OR (DEFICITS) AS A PERCENTAGE OF GDP 1975 – 2015** (in billions) |

| Fiscal Year | GDP | Surplus (Deficit) | Deficit % of GDP | Fiscal Year | GDP | Surplus (Deficit) | Deficit % of GDP |
|---|---|---|---|---|---|---|---|
| 1934 | 61.2 | (3.6) | 5.94% | 1975 | 1,560.2 | (60.7) | 3.89% |
| 1935 | 69.6 | (2.8) | 4.09% | 1976 | 1,738.1 | (76.1) | 4.38% |
| 1936 | 78.5 | (4.5) | 5.69% | 1977 | 1,973.5 | (63.2) | 3.20% |
| 1937 | 87.8 | (2.8) | 3.22% | 1978 | 2,217.5 | (71.9) | 3.24% |
| 1938 | 89.0 | (1.2) | 1.36% | 1979 | 2,501.4 | (59.1) | 2.36% |
| 1939 | 89.1 | (3.9) | 4.37% | 1980 | 2,724.2 | (82.6) | 3.03% |
| 1940 | 96.8 | (4.0) | 4.18% | 1981 | 3,057.0 | (85.8) | 2.81% |
| 1941 | 114.1 | (6.4) | 5.57% | 1982 | 3,223.7 | (134.2) | 4.16% |
| 1942 | 144.3 | (22.5) | 15.59% | 1983 | 3,440.7 | (230.9) | 6.71% |
| 1943 | 180.3 | (57.6) | 31.97% | 1984 | 3,844.4 | (218.3) | 5.68% |
| 1944 | 209.2 | (51.8) | 24.77% | 1985 | 4,146.3 | (266.5) | 6.43% |
| 1945 | 221.4 | (53.0) | 23.93% | 1986 | 4,403.9 | (283.1) | 6.43% |
| 1946 | 222.6 | (19.8) | 8.92% | 1987 | 4,651.4 | (222.3) | 4.78% |
| 1947 | 233.2 | 0.6 | -0.25% | 1988 | 5,008.5 | (252.9) | 5.05% |
| 1948 | 256.6 | 8.8 | -3.44% | 1989 | 5,399.5 | (276.1) | 5.11% |
| 1949 | 271.3 | (1.8) | 0.68% | 1990 | 5,734.5 | (341.2) | 5.95% |
| 1950 | 273.1 | (3.1) | 1.12% | 1991 | 5,930.5 | (381.0) | 6.42% |
| 1951 | 320.2 | 2.5 | -0.77% | 1992 | 6,242.0 | (386.3) | 6.19% |
| 1952 | 348.7 | (5.0) | 1.44% | 1993 | 6,587.3 | (355.4) | 5.40% |
| 1953 | 372.5 | (9.9) | 2.66% | 1994 | 6,976.6 | (298.5) | 4.28% |
| 1954 | 377.0 | (3.2) | 0.84% | 1995 | 7,341.1 | (263.2) | 3.59% |
| 1955 | 395.9 | (4.2) | 1.05% | 1996 | 7,718.3 | (222.1) | 2.88% |
| 1956 | 427.0 | 1.3 | -0.31% | 1997 | 8,211.7 | (147.8) | 1.80% |
| 1957 | 450.9 | 1.7 | -0.37% | 1998 | 8,663.0 | (91.9) | 1.06% |
| 1958 | 460.0 | (3.0) | 0.66% | 1999 | 9,208.4 | (87.1) | 0.95% |
| 1959 | 490.2 | (11.3) | 2.30% | 2000 | 9,821.0 | 1.6 | -0.02% |
| 1960 | 518.9 | 0.8 | -0.15% | 2001 | 10,225.3 | (100.5) | 0.98% |
| 1961 | 529.9 | (4.2) | 0.79% | 2002 | 10,543.9 | (360.2) | 3.42% |
| 1962 | 567.8 | (6.8) | 1.21% | 2003 | 10,980.2 | (556.0) | 5.06% |
| 1963 | 599.2 | (6.6) | 1.11% | 2004 | 11,676.0 | (605.4) | 5.18% |
| 1964 | 641.5 | (8.6) | 1.34% | 2005 | 12,428.6 | (555.1) | 4.47% |
| 1965 | 687.5 | (3.9) | 0.57% | 2006 | 13,206.5 | (537.3) | 4.07% |
| 1966 | 755.8 | (5.2) | 0.68% | 2007 | 13,861.4 | (409.4) | 2.95% |
| 1967 | 810.0 | (15.7) | 1.94% | 2008 | 14,334.4 | (724.6) | 5.06% |
| 1968 | 868.4 | (28.4) | 3.27% | 2009 | 13,960.7 | (1,540.0) | 11.03% |
| 1969 | 948.1 | (4.9) | 0.51% | 2010 | 14,348.4 | (1,416.8) | 9.87% |
| 1970 | 1,012.7 | (13.2) | 1.30% | 2011 | 14,929.4 | (1,396.6) | 9.35% |
| 1971 | 1,080.0 | (29.9) | 2.77% | 2012 | 15,547.4 | (1,176.8) | 7.57% |
| 1972 | 1,176.5 | (29.3) | 2.49% | 2013 | 16,498.1 | (765.9) | 4.64% |
| 1973 | 1,310.6 | (25.7) | 1.96% | 2014 | 17,183.5 | (613.2) | 3.57% |
| 1974 | 1,438.5 | (20.1) | 1.40% | 2015 | 17,803.4 | (550.0) | 3.09% |

Source:  http://www.whitehouse.gov/omb/budget/Historicals/     Source:  http://www.whitehouse.gov/omb/budget/Historicals/

# END NOTES

[1] eszlinger.com website, *Titanic* Facts

[2] cnn.com, March 31, 2015

[3] Bipartisan Budget Act of 2015, H.R. 1314

[4] Congressional Budget and Impoundment Control Act of 1974, H.R. 7130, congress.gov *website*

[5] *The Budget and Economic Outlook, Fiscal Years 2013 to 2014*, cbo.gov *website*

[6] Department of Defense, Select Acquisition Report, RCS: DD-A&T(Q&A)823-198

[7] Congressional Budget and Impoundment Control Act of 1974

[8] www.treasurydirect.gov

[9] Federal Reserve Statistical Release January 2, 2015

[10] Federal Reserve Board website

[11] Ibid

[12] Reuters, August 5, 2013

[13] Fannie and Freddie May Need More Bailouts, Wall Street Journal op-ed, March 31, 2015

[14] Social Security Amendments of 1983, P.L. 98-21

[15] The 2015 Annual Report of the Board of Trustees of the Federal Old-Age and Survivors Insurance and Federal Disability Insurance Trust Funds, published July 22, 2015

[16] Population Reference Bureau website, *Just How Many Baby Boomers Are There?* April 2014

[17] *Impoundment*, American Heritage, December 1973, Volume 25, Issue 1

[18] Impoundment. West's Encyclopedia of American Law, 2005

[19] Fisher, Louis. Congressional Budget and Impoundment Control Act (1974). Major Acts of Congress. 2004 *Encyclopedia.com*

[20] Entin, Jonathan L. Balanced Budget and Emergency Deficit Control Act (1985), Major Acts of Congress. 2004 *Enclyopedia.com*

[21] Statutes on the Congressional Budget Process

[22] Ronald D. Utt, Ph.D. "The Bridge to Nowhere: A National Embarrassment," October 20, 2005, heritage.org

[23] "Reid's Cowboy Poetry Puffery," March 10, 2011, factcheck.org

[24] Kathy Gill. "The 1996 Line Item Veto Act." April 24, 2014, uspolitics.about.com

[25] "The Statutory Pay-As-You-Go Act of 2010: A Description. May 1, 2014, whitehouse.gov

[26] Factcheck.org website, *Medicare's 'Piggy Bank,'* Lori Roberston, August 24, 2012

[27] Bureau of Labor Statistics website *Health Care – Spotlight on Statistics: Chart Data*

[28] Bureau of Economic Analysis website

[29] *Fact Sheet: ACA Risk Sharing Mechanisms*, American Academy of Actuaries, © 2013

[30] *Health Republic Insurance Company v. the United States*

[31] *National Federation of Independent Business v. Sebelius*

[32] IRS IR-2012-4, January 6, 2012

[33] Marketplaces Faced Early Challenges Resolving Inconsistencies With Applicant Data, Department of Health and Human Services, Office of the Inspector General, June 2014 OEI-01-14-0018

[34] Not All Internal Controls Implemented By The Federal, California and Connecticut Marketplaces Were Effective In Ensuring That Individuals Were Enrolled in Qualified Health Plans According To Federal Requirements, Department of Health and Human Services, Office of the Inspector General, June 2014 A-09-14-01000

[35] Patient Protection and Affordable Care Act: Preliminary Results of Undercover Testing of Enrollment Controls for Health Care Coverage and Consumer Subsidies Provided Under the Act, July 23, 2014 GAO-14-705T

[36] Joint Committee on Taxation, Publication JCX-45-12, May 29, 2012